N
645 - 5345

# EUCHARISTIC THEOLOGY

# EUCHARISTIC THEOLOGY

JOSEPH M. POWERS, S.J.

HERDER AND HERDER

1967
HERDER AND HERDER NEW YORK
232 Madison Avenue, New York 10016

*Imprimi potest:* John F. X. Connolly, S.J.
*Nihil obstat:* Leo J. Steady, Censor Librorum
*Imprimatur:* ✠ Robert F. Joyce, Bishop of Burlington
January 5, 1967

Library of Congress Catalog Card Number: 67–17625

Manufactured in the United States

# CONTENTS

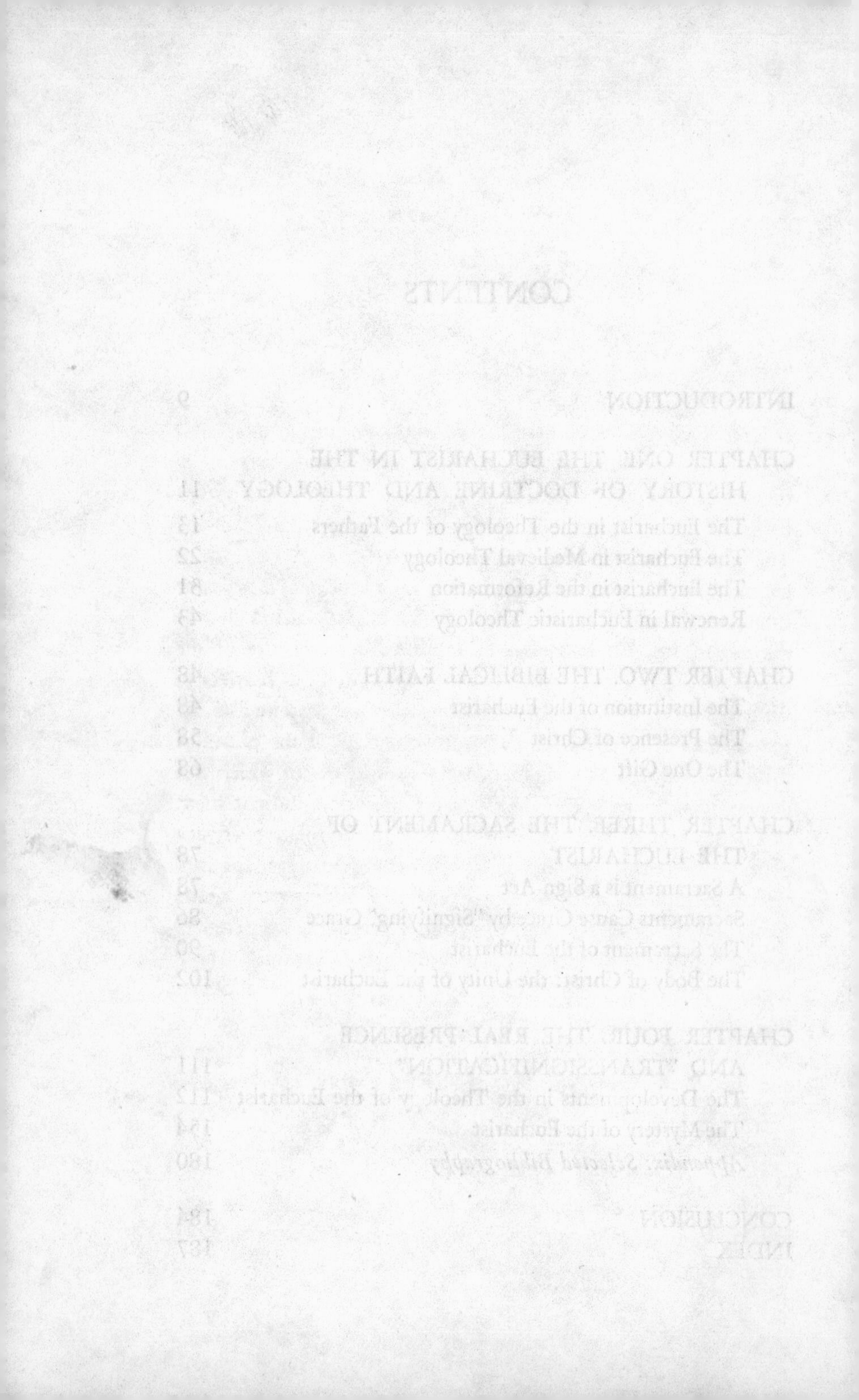

# CONTENTS

# INTRODUCTION

THE publication of the encyclical "Mysterium Fidei" on September 12, 1965, brought to the attention and concern of the Church at large a movement in the theological analysis of the sacrament of the Eucharist which traces back to the annual interconfessional theological discussions held at the Benedictine priory of Saint-Croix d'Amay at Chevetogne, Belgium, September 24–27, 1958. The papers read at that conference were characterized by a genuine theological ecumenism in that the participants laid aside linguistic differences in an attempt to state a very realistic view of the presence of Christ in the Eucharist without the use of the theological shibboleths which have served so long as barriers to Christian unity. The contents of those papers are presented in the fourth chapter of this book. What is important at the outset of this presentation is an awareness of the context out of which this development grew. It grew from a fresh attempt at the statement of Christ's real presence in the Eucharist. In the relative privacy of the conferences, the use of new insights and new language served to promote Christian understanding and respect. Quite soon, however, the publication of the Chevetogne conferences opened a theological debate which is still being continued. Theologians, particularly the Flemish and Dutch theologians, began to analyze the positions taken at Chevetogne from the point of view of the insights and language of contemporary views of man and his world. These writings, printed in Catholic newspapers, devotional magazines and clerical journals, reached a wide audience and began a debate between those who found the new positions incapable of expressing the traditional faith of the Church and those who, perhaps too eagerly, found the new insights so much in keeping with modern man's view of himself and his world.

It must be admitted on the one hand that not every presentation of the traditional faith of the Church in the sacramental reality of the Eucharist has been balanced by situating the reality of Christ's presence in a broad theological context which takes all the dimensions of the Eucharist into consideration. The fruits of this lack of balance can be seen in the "prisoner of the tabernacle" mystique, the fear of biting the host and other oversimplified attitudes toward the unique character of Christ's presence in the action of the Eucharist. On the other hand, however, it must also be admitted that not every presentation of the recent developments has been a good one. One finds a too literal application of human paradigms to the presence of Christ in the Eucharist, an excessive concentration on the presence of Christ devoid of the same broad theological context. Some new presentations, like some old presentations, fall into a univocity which forgets the transcendent difference between the bodily condition of the Risen Jesus and the condition of men in this present life.

Pope Paul's encyclical threads its way between both of these excesses and presents a well-balanced statement on the Eucharist which sets all the dimensions of the Eucharist into a well-focused unity. The encyclical stresses the fact that the Eucharist is a mystery, and that human formulations of it cannot be tied to any cultural or scientific milieu. The statements which the Church has made concerning the Eucharist are to be understood as statements which correspond to the ordinary experience of ordinary men. True, the statement of the faith of the Church can be developed and clarified, but these developments and clarifications are not to be seen as the exclusive property of any particular school of thought. To the extent that they state the faith of the Church, they must be seen as corresponding to the understanding of men of every age and of every cultural background. Thus, the encyclical admits the value of the new language, but calls for a full appreciation of the deep realism of the Church's faith in the Eucharist, the realism of her faith in Christ's presence, the realism of her faith in the fact that bread and wine are changed into the reality of Christ, the reality of the sacrificial character of the Eucharist and of the ecclesial character of every celebration of the Eucharist, the realism of the sacramental symbolism of the Eucharist as sign and cause of the unity of the Church.

It is in the spirit of this deep realism of the faith of the Church that these pages are presented. In the spirit of the encyclical, they attempt to situate the question of the real presence of Christ in its biblical and historical context, showing how differences in the experience of the Eucharistic celebration itself have led to differences in the emphasis which has been placed on the various dimensions of the totality of the Eucharist. The presentation then returns to the biblical faith, the ultimate controlling factor of the Church's belief. Rather than concentrating on the narrow question of the real presence of Christ, the presentation of the biblical faith seeks to show how that question is situated in a broader context of the sacrificial reality, the unity of the Church, and the timeless priesthood of Christ. From this there flow a number of sacramental considerations which form the third chapter. Finally, the new developments are presented in a bibliographical survey from the time of the Chevetogne conference until the present.

The purpose of this presentation is to inform. Most of the recent writings are written in Dutch, a language not commonly read in the American theological community, but a language whose importance is increasing continuously. In the absence of the ability to read this literature, one finds distortions of positions and a discouraging lack of appreciation of what is actually being said. It is hoped that this presentation will make clear the orthodoxy of the intentions and content of most of this literature. The burden of this literature is an attempt to reach an ecumenical understanding of the mystery of the Eucharist as well as the deepening of the faith of Catholics in this central treasure of faith. One can only hope that this presentation will serve these same purposes.

It is trite to say that this is an age of dialogue. The dialogue is a necessity of the times, when mankind is coming closer and closer into unity, but into a unity where differences are all the more troubling because of man's proximity to man. In this age of the life of the Church and of the world in which it lives, the very closeness of people who were once separated by chasms of geography and culture demands greater understanding and fairness on the part of those who, willingly or unwillingly, are being brought together, in God's providence, by man's ingenuity. One might hope that the charity of Christ would be the guiding principle of men's dealings with one another, but even that hope must be tempered by the acknowledging of the fact that individual and cultural differences do not melt away, even in the most sincere attempts at dialogue. These differences are coming more and more into the consciousness of the Church. It is becoming more and more apparent that unity does not demand an absolute uniformity. Rather, it demands a common commitment to the truth of Christ which, instead of being possessed by any one man, possesses all men and calls all to its faithful service.

CHAPTER ONE

# THE EUCHARIST IN THE HISTORY OF DOCTRINE AND THEOLOGY

THE Holy Eucharist is a mystery. But, as one aspect of the sacramental dispensation of salvation, it is a mystery which is placed by God into the visible continuity of human history. And, as a genuinely historical reality, its exterior shape has shared in the variations which are an essential part of the historical. From the origins of the Church until our own time, the forms in which the Eucharist has been celebrated have varied from time to time and from place to place, and in our own time this one mystery continues to be celebrated in a variety of forms in the variety of traditions which continue to live in the Church.

As commonplace as this may appear, it is still noteworthy because this diversity in the shape of the Eucharist has produced a corresponding diversity of theological attitudes. Reflecting on different experiences of the Eucharist, theologians of different traditions have emphasized and continue to emphasize different aspects of this extremely rich sacramental action. In our own time, for example, the presence of the epiklesis in the liturgies of the eastern rites and its absence in the western rites still creates a basic difference of approach and of emphasis in the theological treatment of the Eucharist. Likewise, the closed iconostasis screen of the eastern Church creates an experience of the Eucharist as the *"mysterium tremendum,"* a worship which is not seen, but one which is heard with deep reverence. The western liturgy has preserved the "open" character of the Eucharist as the celebration in which the community as a whole is called to take part, thus granting the gradual clericalization of the Eucharist, as this brief study will show. Therefore, the historical interaction of liturgical experience, theological emphasis and Eucharistic piety (or its lack) calls for a brief historical sketch whose function will be to highlight the evolution in the theology and Christian piety which have centered around the evolution in the shape of the celebration of the Eucharist from the beginnings until the present.

The function of this indication of theological and doctrinal evolution is by no means the establishment of a theological relativism which would admit everything without discretion. Quite to the contrary, the purpose here is to point out the faith in the Eucharist which has always been one and the same in the Church, this even amid significant changes of theological and doctrinal perspective. This is what Pope Paul VI has called for in his encyclical on the teaching and worship of the Eucharist: that in the midst of variations in practice "we might rejoice in the faith of the Church which has always been one and the same."[1] For this reason, then, our intention is to trace briefly the origins of the attitudes which confront one another at this time. And one of the problems of this period in the history of the Church, indeed of every period of significant change in the life of the Church, is a type of fundamentalist interpretation of the teaching of the Church which would project contemporary attitudes on past ages and attempt to root present attitudes and problems in times when neither these attitudes nor these problems existed.[2]

The purpose of this survey, then, is to draw back from the alienation of questions which has taken place in the history of

1. "Mysterium fidei, Litt. encycl. de doctrina et cultu ss. Eucharistiae," in *AAS* 57 (1965), p. 770.

2. See, for example, G. Bareille's study "L'Eucharistie d'apres les Pères," in *DTC,* 15, 1, coll. 1121–1183. Bareille's explicit concern is consciously restricted to an investigation of the real presence and of the doctrine of transsubstantiation in patristic theology. By way of contrast, J. Betz's study "Eucharistie" in *Handbuch Theologischer Grundbegriffe,* vol. 1, pp. 336–355, gives a broader and more adequate treatment of the theology of the Fathers without worrying about the later questions of real presence and transsubstantiation.

theology and to resituate the problems where they belong, viz., in the historical moment in which they arose. For it is in the emergence of theological problems in a definite historical context that the questions are clear. The alienation of a question takes place in the fundamentalism of later ages which read the questions incorrectly and, in a fundamentalist transfer of language and attitudes, distort the real import of historical questions. For this reason, if in E. Schillebeeckx's words "our faith is a faith in *historicity*," our reëvaluation of the questions of theology will not terminate in a panicky relativism, but in a clearly perspectived and calm appreciation of the very particular character of history.[3]

## *The Eucharist in the Theology of the Fathers*

The first six centuries after Christ were the greatest period of development in the shape of the Eucharistic celebration. The gathering of the Christians to celebrate the Eucharist grew from the simple domestic celebrations to the elaborate papal liturgies of the 6th and 7th centuries which transferred the splendor of the imperial court to the Christian basilica. The reconstructions of the earliest forms of the Eucharist present a domestic Eucharist not very different from the more solemn religious family gatherings which were characteristic of the Jewish liturgical calendar. The prayer of thanksgiving into which the elements of the present canon are inserted followed upon scriptural readings and blessings which can be seen to be rooted in meal-celebrations such as the *Seder* of the Jewish Passover. With the Edict of Toleration in the 4th century, the celebration of the Eucharist took on a more "official" character. The celebration took place in the *basilica,* the official gathering place for Christians as it was for the Roman political body. The bishop was seated on a throne like the Roman magistrate. The ceremony eventually became more elaborate with the introduction of the cycle of feasts, the Kyrie-litany and the prayers of the presiding prelate over gifts and

3. "Transsubstantiation, Transfinalization, Transsignification," in *Worship* 40 (1966), pp. 324–325.

people. Gradually, a fixed outline for the canon emerged which, though still left to the improvising capacities of the individual bishop or celebrant, came to include a set number of elements into which the words of consecration were set.

Likewise, though the office of priest had been in existence since the late first or early second century, it was not the function of the priest to preside at the celebration of the Eucharist. The place for the priest was in the priests' choir, the *presbyterium,* not at the altar, unless he was delegated to celebrate by the bishop. And since the canon had no really fixed form, it was the bishop alone who pronounced the words of the canon. It was the priest's function to assist the bishop to the extent that this was necessary or desirable in the preparation of the offerings, the breaking of the bread and the distribution of communion. Only with the growth of Christianity to numbers which demanded more than one church in a city did the "titular" or parish church come into existence as the "title" for the ordination of a given priest, who was ordained to serve the bishop in a given church; the number of priests depended on the real Eucharistic needs of a given city. And even in these parish churches, the Eucharist was celebrated only as a conscious extension of the Eucharist of the bishop. This is all still present in the Roman liturgy in the dismissal: *Ite, missa est,* which does not mean "Go, the Mass is ended," but "Go, for the Eucharist *has been sent* to the titular churches for their Eucharist."[4] It is also present in the dropping of a portion of the host into the chalice after the consecration, a gesture once meant to convey that the consecration takes place because this particle from the bishop's Eucharist is placed among the offerings of this community as the "yeast" (*fermentum*) which makes this Eucharist one with his.[5]

By the beginning of the 6th century the main lines of the Eucharist as it is known today in the West were solidified. At the same time, the specific liturgies of the East had developed into their classical lines due to the influence of great centers of

4. H. Schmidt, S.J., *Introductio in Liturgiam Occidentalem,* Rome, 1960. P. 410.

5. J. C. McGowan, R.S.C.J., *Concelebration,* New York, 1964. P. 27.

learning and influence such as Alexandria and Antioch. The development in the West during the 6th and 7th centuries consisted in a greater assimilation of liturgical forms to the practices of the Roman imperial court, the use of the ceremonial handkerchief (the maniple), the adoption of the chasuble, the ritual procession of entrance, the rank of sub-deacon, and the origins of a fixed style of prayer and chant.

In the midst of this evolution and variation, however, one constant factor emerges. This is the fact that the experience of the Eucharist was always a communitarian experience. The paradigm around which the theological reflection of the Fathers of Christian teaching centered was the celebration of the Eucharist by the whole of the Christian community in a given city or parish. Indeed, the emphasis on the unity of the community celebrating the Eucharist was so strong that only one celebration was permitted on each altar and only one altar was permitted in each Church. It was only in the 5th century that it became acceptable to celebrate another Mass for those who could not be present at the Eucharist of the bishop, indeed even to celebrate at the bishop's altar.[6] But even here, the basic consideration was the fact that not everyone could fit into the bishop's church for the bishop's Eucharist. Thus, the image of the Eucharist which formed the basis of theological reflection was one of the Eucharist celebrated by the entire Christian community assembled together around the bishop who, in turn, was surrounded by his choir of priests. The bishop celebrated the Eucharist, but the community was seen as concelebrating with him, each according to his rank in the community, deacons and priests assisting at the altar as needed, the congregation joining the choir in antiphonal chants and processional hymns, but all celebrating the one Eucharist.

Thus, the primary emphasis in the theology of the Eucharist from the beginning was the fact that the Eucharist is the image and source of the unity of the Christian community. This is the emphasis stressed repeatedly by Ignatius of Antioch (*Eph.* 4, 5; *Trall.* 7, 2), as in his insistence on the very validity of the Eucharist depending on the presence or permission of the bishop:

6. *Ibid.*

Let no one do anything touching the Church apart from the bishop. Let that celebration of the Eucharist be considered valid which is held under the bishop or anyone to whom he has committed it. Where the bishop appears, there let the people be, just as where Jesus Christ is, there is the Catholic Church. It is not permitted without authorization from the bishop either to baptize or to hold an *agapé;* but whatever he approves is also pleasing to God. Thus everything you do will be proof against danger and valid. [*Smyrn.* 8]

But the meaning of the Eucharist was also presented as extending beyond the individual Christian communities and encompassing the image of the entire Church. This is made clear in the image of Roman concelebrations as early as the 3rd and 4th centuries in the description of the bishops concelebrating with the Pope on their visits to Rome. The *Didascalia* gave instructions that visiting priests were to be received into the presbyterium of other places with honor while the laity were to be questioned by the deacon if they were married or widowed, whether they belonged to the Church and were not heretics, and thus be assigned their due place in the Church. But a bishop was to be seated with the bishop of the place visited, was asked to deliver a sermon to the faithful and to pray the canon. But if, out of deference, he refused to pray the whole canon, he was to speak the consecration over the chalice.[7] The canons of other local synods of the 3rd and 4th centuries also state the right of bishops visiting Rome to be seated with other bishops at the papal Eucharist.[8] This practice seems to have extended at least until the 10th century.[9]

Thus, the Eucharist is the very image of the unity of the Church, the visible sign that bishops, priests and laity alike are members of the communion of the Church, and the testimony to the orthodoxy of their status and teaching. And it is in this context that the statements of the real presence of Christ, the change in the bread and wine are to be found. These latter questions were of no great concern in and of themselves to the period of the Fathers. They are only mentioned in the broader

7. *Didascalia,* II, 58, 3. Ed. Funke, pp. 166, 168.
8. McGowan, *op. cit.,* pp. 25–26.
9. *Ibid.,* pp. 26–35.

context of the Eucharist as the sign and source of the life of the Church.

This does not mean, however, that the teaching of the real presence and of the change of the bread and wine is not to be found in the Fathers. It means rather that this teaching is to be found rather in the context of the Eucharist as the source of the life and unity of the community. Thus, Ignatius of Antioch states the real presence clearly enough, but his principal emphasis is unity:

> From the Eucharist and prayer they [Docetists] hold aloof, because they do not confess that the Eucharist is the flesh of our saviour Jesus Christ, which suffered for our sins and which the Father in his loving-kindness raised from the dead. [*Smyrn.* 7]
>
> It is proper, therefore, to avoid associating with such people and not to speak about them either in private or in public. . . . You must all follow the lead of the bishop as Jesus Christ followed that of the Father. . . . [*Smyrn.* 7–8]

The principal objection of the Docetists to the Eucharist was not any problem with the real presence itself, but the more basic problem of the humanity of Jesus (see *Smyrn.* 5). Irenaeus took up the same argument in his attack on the Gnostics (*Adv. Haer.* 4, 18; 5, 2). In the persecutions at Carthage (*c.* 250), Cyprian was enraged because those who had abandoned the unity of the Church or had been baptized into heretical sects had been admitted to the Eucharist. This does violence to the very body and blood of Christ, even more so than when these people denied Christ (*Epist.* 75). But when the persecution was renewed (*c.* 260), he admitted those who had repented to the Eucharist so that they might be strengthened in unity through the body and blood of Christ, "for how can they be expected to shed their blood for Christ unless they themselves are granted to share in His blood?" (*Epist.* 67). Once again, the emphasis is not on the fact of the real presence itself, but on the meaning of the real presence of Christ: the nourishment of the Church and the Christian in time of persecution.

Another valuable patristic source for the theology of the Eucharist is to be found in the *mystagoge,* the catechetical instructions given to those baptized during the Easter and Pentecost vigils. During the week after Easter a series of instructions was given to the neophyte Christians on the meaning of the ceremonies of initiation, Baptism, Confirmation and Eucharist. Two of the most complete of these catecheses have survived in the *Catechetical Orations* of Cyril of Jerusalem (d. 386) and the *De Mysteriis* of Ambrose (d. 397). Commenting on 1 Corinthians 11, 23, Cyril explains the meaning of communion to the neophytes. From the moment that Christ says "This is my body" and "This is my blood" the bread and wine are truly changed into His body and blood so that the Christian becomes one with Him in body and blood, con-corporal and consanguineous. And thus the Christian becomes really a "bearer of Christ" (*Christophoros*) because His body is one and His one blood flows through all (*Cat.* 22, 3). Ambrose emphasizes the reality of the presence of Christ in the context of his description of the splendor of the ceremonies of Baptism and the reception of the Eucharist by the newly baptized. He stresses that this is truly the flesh and blood of Christ, present here by the power of Christ's word, and thus the nourishment of the Church and the Christian (*De Myst.* 9). Both catecheses stress the reality of the presence of Christ, but once again, this is stressed in the context of the solemnity of the reception of the Eucharist, the sacrament by which Christ nourishes His Church. And all this development is against the background of the solemn incorporation of the neophyte into the community of the Church through ceremonies of initiation which are rich in the symbols of unity.

Augustine's (d. 430) theology of the Eucharist is a "problem" for many theologians. The difficulty is not to be found in his lack of statements of the doctrine of the real presence. Rather, it is found in the fact that his theology of the Eucharist is far more comprehensive than the statement of the fact of the real presence. His sermons, letters and other writings abound with statements such as

> The bread which you see on the altar, once it is sanctified by the word of God, is the body of Christ. And that chalice, or rather what

the chalice contains, once it is sanctified by the word of God, is the blood of Christ. [*Serm.* 227]

This is a perfectly clear statement of the fact of the real presence of the body and blood of Christ, a presence which is the result of the words of consecration. Without any philosophical elaboration, it is a clear and simple statement of the traditional belief of the Church at his time.

In spite of these clear statements, however, Augustine worries some theologians because of the sacramental context into which he sets the real presence. Thus, as van der Lof indicates, given the multiplicity of meanings in which Augustine uses the word "*sacramentum,*" some are disconcerted when he applies this word to the body and blood of Christ.[10] On the one hand, it is true that expressions such as "*sacramentum corporis*" and "*sacramentum sanguinis*" indicate the sacred species under which Christ is truly present. Thus in the *De Trinitate,* after distinguishing the ways in which Christ is present in the works of St. Paul (in his preaching, letters, in the sacrament of His body and blood), Augustine makes a sharp distinction between these different meanings of *sacramentum:*

. . . but we do not say that his tongue, nor his parchments nor the ink, nor the meaningful sounds which come from his tongue, nor the marks of the letters as they are written by pens are the body and blood of the Lord; this is only to be found in that which has been taken from the fruits of the earth, consecrated by the prayer of the mystery and rightly received for our spiritual health in memory of the Lord's suffering for us. [III, iv, 10]

In other words, the body and blood of the Lord are only present in their strictest sacramental sense when we receive the consecrated bread and wine of the Eucharist. What is important in the Eucharist, however, is not the physical fact of the real presence, but the fact that the really present Christ is received in the commemoration of His suffering for us. Christ is adored, as van

10. "Eucharistie et présence réelle selon S. Augustin (à propos d'un commentaire sur 'De civitate Dei,' X, vi)," in *Revue des Etudes Augustiniennes,* 10 (1964), p. 298.

der Meer remarks, not as a permanently reserved Host, but He is adored in the reverent handling and reception of the "sacrament" of His body and blood, the Eucharistic Species. It is under these appearances, in these *signs* that Christ is present to be received for the salvation of the Christian.[11]

Van der Lof indicates another "tension" in Augustine's language which also disconcerts some theologians. This is a tension which arises once again from the sacramental context into which Augustine sets his treatment of the Eucharist. This full sacramental context is particularly striking in two sermons to the newly baptized. In the first, an Easter sermon to the newly baptized, he states:

> You should know what you have received, what you will receive, what you should receive daily. The bread which you see on the altar, when it has been sanctified by the word of God, is the body of Christ. . . . If you have received it rightly, you are what you have received. For the Apostle says: because there is one loaf, we who are many are one body (1 Cor. 10, 17). This is how he explained the sacrament of the Lord's table. [*Serm.* 227; *PL* 38, 1099–1100]

Again, in a Pentecost sermon to the newly baptized:

> . . . how is the bread His body? And the chalice, or rather what the chalice contains, how is it His blood? Brethren, these things are called *sacramenta* because in them one thing is seen, but something else is understood. What is seen has a bodily appearance, but what is understood has a spiritual fruitfulness. Thus, if you wish to understand the body of Christ, listen to the Apostle, who says to the believers: You are the body of Christ and His members (1 Cor 12, 27). And thus, if you are the body of Christ and His members, it is your mystery which has been placed on the altar of the Lord; you receive your own mystery. You answer "Amen" to what you are, and in answering, you accept it. For you hear, "The body of Christ" and you answer "Amen." Be a member of Christ's body, so that your Amen may be true. [*Serm.* 272; *PL* 38, 1246–1247]

Thus the expression that the body of Christ is present in the Eucharist *in figura* (in a figure), *in signo* (in a sign), *in sacramento* (in a sacrament) does not mean that Christ is only

11. *Saint Augustin, pasteur d'âmes,* Paris, 1955. Cited in van der Lof, *art. cit.*, p. 296.

symbolically present. It means, as has been seen, that Christ is present in the species of bread and wine which are the sign of His true corporal presence and it means that this true corporal presence is, in turn, a *sacramentum,* the sign and cause of a further grace-reality which is the very continuing existence of the Church as Christ's body. In other words, the real presence of Christ is not the ultimate value in the Eucharist. The ultimate value of this presence is the unity of the Church brought about in the sacramental commemoration of the Passion of Christ in the reception of Christ under the species of bread and wine.

If some authors find problems and disconcerting statements in Augustine's theology of the Eucharist, it would seem that these problems arise not so much from Augustine's theology itself, but rather from the fact that some theologians limit their study of Augustine on this topic to the mere statement of the real presence. Augustine states that presence quite clearly, both directly and by implication, but he situates the real presence in the context of a full and adequate theology of the Eucharist, a theology which goes beyond the mere statement of real presence by transsubstantiation to include the full sacramental meaning and power of that presence and change.

If nothing has been mentioned in this brief survey concerning the theoretical explanation of the change of bread and wine into the body and blood of Christ, it is because there is no such theoretical treatment in the theology of the Fathers. There is a variety of expressions which attempt to describe this change: transmutation, transfiguration, transelementation, transformation. But the basic import of these expressions is the fact that what seems to be bread and wine is in actuality the body and blood of Christ. When the Fathers come to the question of how the bread and wine are changed, their answer is simply that the change is brought about by God's power. Ambrose insists that if the word of Christ is powerful enough to bring into existence what did not exist, it is obviously powerful enough to change what already exists into something else (*De Myst.* 52).

Cyril of Jerusalem and perhaps Augustine reflect the liturgical surroundings of the change when they attribute the change to the power and operation of the Holy Spirit. Augustine cites this operation in his presentation of the ways in which God uses human instruments to bring about spiritual effects:

> And although this [sacrament of the body and blood of Christ] is brought to its visible form by the hands of men, it is not sanctified so that it is the great sacrament except the Spirit of God be invisibly at work. [*De Trin.* III, iv]

And Cyril reflects the liturgical usage of the East more clearly:

> Then, after we have sanctified ourselves by the singing of this holy song [Holy, Holy, Holy, . . .], we pray that the merciful God will send His Holy Spirit over the gifts lying before Him so that He [the Holy Spirit] might make the bread the body of Christ and the wine the blood of Christ, because if the Holy Spirit touches anything, it is surely sanctified and changed. [*Cat.* 23, 7; *PG* 33, 1116]

But even here, Cyril does not stop at the fact of real presence. He adduces this true sanctification and change as the reason why the neophyte should handle the Eucharist carefully and with great reverence.

After Augustine's formulation of the theology of the Eucharist, the history of this theology became "conservative" in character. From the 6th to the 9th century, the turbulence of the great migrations put an end to the creative work of the great Fathers of Christian teaching and the preservative work of the growing monastic movement saved the teaching of the early Church for later generations. At the same time, two different emphases, Eucharistic "realism," stressing the reality of the change in the bread and wine, and Eucharistic "spiritualism," stressing the sacramental character of the Eucharist in the Augustinian sense, became fixed positions which erupted into controversy with the coming of the Carolingian renaissance.

### *The Eucharist in Medieval Theology*

The "middle ages" usually brings to mind the vision of the splendor of Gothic cathedrals, the flowering of great universities such as Oxford and Paris, the brilliance of the great medieval doctors such as Thomas Aquinas, Bonaventure, Scotus, Albert the Great. But the brilliance of the 13th century was the culmination and synthesis of a long and somewhat chaotic development which had its beginnings in the renaissance of the 9th century and the evolution of the structure of Europe and European civilization as it has come to be known. The understanding of the Eucharistic theology of the middle ages, then, demands a brief (and necessarily simplified) description of the evolution of the shape of the Eucharist into its medieval form and of the evolution of the theology of the Eucharist which accompanied this liturgical development.

The period between the 8th and 11th centuries, a period whose tremendous intellectual, political and liturgical activity is generally ignored in theological studies, is variously described as "the dark ages," "the age of iron" or "the age of the formation of Europe." And from the point of view of the old Roman empire, they were dark ages indeed. The political and religious chaos in Rome coupled with the conversion and consolidation of northern Europe conspired to relocate the religious and intellectual center of Christendom from the Eternal City to the courts of the New Roman Empire at Aachen and the other palaces of Charlemagne. One cannot help but find Leo III's gesture in crowning Charlemagne emperor of the West at once courageous and poignant in its recognition of the death of the old order and the birth of the new.

The Eucharistic liturgy of 9th-century northern Europe has been described as "Romanized Celtic."[12] Its origins are not completely Roman, —indeed, it bears, along with the penitential practice of the Celts, the stamp of the East more than that of the West. The roots of this characteristic are easily enough seen in the presence and influence of Alcuin of York at the court of Charlemagne. Indeed, it was Alcuin more than perhaps anyone else who helped to shape the Carolingian reform in letters and liturgy alike. But Alcuin was the product of a tradition which is easily traced to the forms and spirit of the eastern monastic

12. J. Jungmann, S.J., *The Mass of the Roman Rite,* New York and London, 1951. Vol. I, p. 76.

institutions. For he was a product of the monastic traditions of southern France transplanted into the British Isles, only to return to the continent in the great missionary efforts of the conversion of northern Europe. Rather than being characterized by the almost laconic sobriety and dignity of the Roman liturgy, the Eucharistic worship of northern Europe was fond of long, repetitious and numerous prayers. From this period there come elements of the Roman rite which persist to this day: the use of "I" rather than "we" in Mass prayers, progressively longer periods of silent prayer by the celebrant, the addition of frequent protestations of unworthiness on the part of the celebrant and the congregation ("apologies"), a cult of sacred objects which were incensed frequently during the Eucharist, and, in general, a more emotional and affected Eucharistic piety. H. Schmidt refers to this type of Eucharist as the "*missa affectus*" (the Mass of affection or emotion),[13] and points out the elements of our Mass which date from this period, among which are the confession and other prayers before Mass, the use of unleavened bread, the multiplicity of incensation, the silent canon, the multiplication of signs of the cross during the canon prayers, the custom of receiving communion kneeling, and the blessing.

But perhaps of even greater importance than these less sober manifestations of piety and their effects on the simple clarity of the Roman Eucharistic liturgy is the fact that the Eucharist was no longer celebrated consciously as an action of the Christian community. A number of factors contributed to the fact that the Eucharist became a clerical preserve. One factor was the simple matter of language. Out of their esteem for things Roman as signs of authentic culture, the men of the 8th and 9th centuries abhorred translating either the Mass or the scriptures into the now dominant Romance dialects. Thus only the clergy and the educated classes could really understand what the Eucharistic prayers were saying. Further, Isidore of Seville's prevalent sacramental theology presented the sacrament as a "sacred secret," a stress which was accented even more by the silence of the canon and many other prayers of the celebrant. The emphasis on the

13. *Op. cit., pp.* 360–363.

divinity of Christ and the consequent phenomenon of prayer being addressed to Him, rather than being addressed to the Father through Him, coupled with the frequent protestations of unworthiness, emphasized the Eucharist as the *mysterium tremendum,* and the primitive admonition that "holy things are for the holy" took on the meaning that the Christian community was itself unworthy of its Eucharist and that the community's place is at a distance from the Eucharistic action. No longer was the Eucharist placed in the hands of the communicants (who, responding logically to the "apologies" of the liturgy, became fewer and fewer), and when the Eucharist was received, it was received not in the traditional posture of Christian prayer, standing, but in a posture of servility, on one's knees.

The clerical emphasis in the Eucharist had a number of other causes besides those just mentioned. Since at least the 7th century, the Popes permitted the great monastic institutions to ordain larger and larger numbers of their monks. This was certainly essential for the evangelization of northern Europe and the British Isles. This was the work of the priest-monks, under the leadership of such men as Columban, Boniface and Augustine. After the great missionary ages of the 6th century and following, great communities of monks flourished in the north of Europe and the British Isles. And the Eucharist of the monastic orders and cathedral chapters, though still a community celebration for monks and canons, co-existed with the private Mass, the personal devotion of the priest. Further, during the great plagues of later centuries, the foundation of chantries and Mass-chapels displayed the Eucharist more and more as the personal function of the priest. This attitude was fortified by the architecture of the time. The altar was taken from the midst of the community, placed against the rear wall of the apse, separated from the congregation first by the choir of the clergy and eventually by the rood screen. Thus, the piety of the laity at Mass necessarily became one of worshipping from afar, adoring the distant Eucharist rather than actively participating in and receiving the Eucharist as their "daily bread." This is the form of the Eucharist which eventually became the Roman paradigm for celebration when, in the 11th century, the Popes looked to the Frankish kingdoms for rituals, importing them into a Rome which was almost at the bottom of its cultural and religious resources.

Thus, a Eucharistic liturgy developed which was almost totally foreign to the Roman Mass of the 4th and 5th centuries. In those times, the community itself was the focus of the celebration, this to the extent that in the liturgy of the Roman basilica, the altar itself was only a table brought into the presbyterium when it came time for the Eucharistic prayers and offerings. Now the altar became a stage on which a sacred drama took place and the function of the congregation was that of observing the sacred action. Indeed, the Eucharistic piety of the 11th century and later consisted primarily in gazing on the elevated Host, the act of adoration which was the source of most of the "fruits" of the Mass. And these "fruits" as they are presented in some of the more popular devotional treatments are quite remarkable: one does not grow older while one attends Mass; the souls in purgatory do not suffer while one offers Mass for them; a woman who gives birth on the day she attends Mass will have a son. It is no wonder that the faithful moved from altar to altar in the great churches to see the elevation. Fortescue tells of the cries of the English which were heard if the Host was not elevated high enough: "Hold up, Sir John, hold up. Heave it a little higher!"[14]

The evolution in the shape of the Mass of the Roman rite and the popular piety which surrounded it was accompanied by a significant shift of emphasis in the theology of the Eucharist in the 9th century. Whereas the theology of the Fathers centered around the community celebration of the Eucharist, the theology of the 8th century and following adopted a more dialectical point of departure centering its attention on the nature of Christ's presence in the Eucharistic Species. And with this change of perspective there began a series of controversies which gave birth to a vast literature of tractates on the body and blood of the Lord, the Sacrament of the altar, the Mystery of the altar, etc. The

14. A. Fortescue, *The Mass. A Study of the Roman Liturgy,* London, 1912, pp. 341 ff. See Jungmann, *op. cit.,* vol. I, pp. 120 ff.; A. Franz, *Die Messe im deutschen Mittelalter,* Freiburg, 1902. Pp. 36 ff.

controversies centered around particular points of the theology of the Eucharist, but this is only one phase of the confrontation of the emerging intellectualism of the dialecticians and the strong conservatism of those who opposed the use of "philosophy" in the treatment of the mystery of faith. It should be remembered, at the same time, that the "philosophy" prevalent in the 8th to the 10th centuries was not the intellectual analysis which has come to be known as "philosophy." Rather, it was basically a grammatical style of analysis of scripture and patristic traditions with a strong bent for the allegorical and moralizing. And if positions on the theology of the Eucharist met with opposition in these centuries, it is not the opposition of different schools of intellectual conviction so much as the clash of dialectic with the sayings of the Fathers and of scripture.

Thus, in the 9th century, Amalarius, the disciple of Alcuin, proposed three different meanings for the expression "body of Christ" and took the position that the body of Christ present in the Eucharist is not the same as the heavenly body of Christ. His point seems to have been not the denial of the identity of these realities but the fact that we do not mean quite the same thing when we speak of one and of the other. What Amalarius meant is not of such great importance, however, as is the fact that his treatment of the Eucharist occasioned a rash of treatises on the Eucharist, one commenting on or opposing the other, during the next two hundred years. And it was in this discussion that the forces of Eucharistic realism and symbolism came to their sharpest confrontation. This was a period of great intellectual growth with the gradual introduction of Aristotle into western thought, an entrance which signalled the eventual death of the influence of Augustine as the master of the theological thought-form. Augustine's teachings were revered, but the style of thinking was completely changed.

It was Augustine's theology of the Eucharist which was perhaps the basic reason for the difficulties of the man who brings the Eucharistic controversies of the 8th to 10th centuries to their climax: Berengar of Tours (d. 1088). Amid Augustine's clear affirmations of the traditional doctrine of the Eucharist his emphasis on the sacramental character of the Eucharist has been shown as giving the real presence a broader scope of meaning. This broader scope was ignored in Berengar's emphasis on Augustine's definition of the sacrament as a "sign of a sacred thing." Not that this was uppermost in Berengar's mind. His theology was, from the outset, subordinate to his logical and grammatical analysis. In his crude pre-nominalist theory of knowledge, Berengar could not distinguish between reality and appearance, insisting that the mind saw things in their very essence and that therefore what was seen was the very essence of things. Thus, if what is seen on the altar is bread, it is bread. And for this reason, no true change in the bread can be affirmed in the Eucharist. This was his basic argument, an argument from his philosophy. As confirmation, he insisted on the definition of the sacrament which comes from Augustine: the sign of a sacred thing. But while in Augustine, and in patristic theology in general, this meant that God truly comes into man's life by assuming earthly things into the dispensation of grace, for Berengar this meant that the material elements are only abstract signs of God's action on the believer. Where sign and reality were equated with one another in the sacramental order in the theology of the Fathers, Berengar (and his contemporaries) opposed the sign and the reality to one another. This is clear not only in Bergengar but in the bizarre Eucharistic realism of the oath of the Roman Synod of 1059 which Berengar was forced to sign:

> . . . [the list of Berengar's errors]. Moreover, I agree with the Holy Roman . . . See, and I profess . . . that I hold that faith . . . which this sacred synod . . . has presented to me to be held . . . namely, that the bread and wine which are placed on the altar, after the consecration, are not simply the sacrament, but the true body and blood of . . . Jesus Christ, and that they are *sensibly,* not only in a sacrament, but *in truth, handled* and *broken* by the hands of the priest, *torn* by the teeth of the faithful, and I swear this . . . [DS 690].

Whatever Berengar might have replied to this statement of the "faith of the Church," he devoted his efforts at reply to a nit-picking logical and grammatical analysis of the propositions of Cardinal Humbert, stating that, if a change took place in the consecration, the proposition "The bread and wine are the body and blood of Christ" makes no sense, because what is said to be the body and blood of Christ (the bread and wine) no longer exists. In other words, there remained no subject for Humbert's predicate. It is only with the more qualified reply of Lanfranc that the faith of the Church was adequately stated. Lanfranc said that this change is completely mysterious, and that while the body of Christ remains in heaven whole, inviolate and uninjured, at the same time it is truly present on the altar. Thus, he clearly distinguished between different ways in which the body of Christ exists: in the Eucharist, in heaven and in the Church.

Other elements of the theology of Eucharist also emerged from this controversy. Berengar ridiculed the extreme realists by stating that they maintained that the body of Christ was scattered in little pieces over the altar. In reply, Lanfranc insisted that the whole Christ was present in every host and every particle. But problems arose from the excessively physical treatment of the Eucharist. Lanfranc's followers, Alger of Liège and Guitmund of Aversa, insisted that the Eucharist was incorruptible, being the body of Christ, and thus there arose those crude medieval positions which maintained that the Eucharistic Species were not digested, and that thus the body of Christ followed the natural cycle of ingestion and elimination of the human organism. Others raised the question which became classical in the middle ages: What does the mouse eat when it gets into the tabernacle and consumes the Eucharistic Host? Answers to this question are many and marvelous, but the more balanced theologians such as Peter Lombard will simply say, "*Deus novit*" (God knows!).

The period following the Berengarian controversy on the real presence, it should be remembered, was the period of the entrance of Aristotle into western philosophy and theology. The reasons for this entrance are various and not of importance to this study. What is important is the fact that this entrance gave a new vocabulary and thought-forms to western theology. It eventually led to the style of thought and theological method which is called "scholastic" theology. The language of Aristotle was gradually incorporated into the dialectical procedure of the medieval thinkers so that both the theological "questions" and the language in which they were framed took on a new appearance. History and dialectics produced a rather standard treatment of the Eucharist as a theological question: the true presence, the true change which takes place in the consecration, the manner of Christ's presence in the Eucharist. These became the questions which comprised the theological treatment of the Eucharist. By the time of Peter Lombard, the basic procedural structure of theology was established to the extent that almost every great theologian included a commentary on Peter Lombard's *Book of Sentences* among his writings. This was the basic textbook in the theological schools well into the 16th century, and the function of the master of theology was to comment on, to agree or disagree with what Peter had written in the 12th century.

It was somewhere in the early third of the 12th century that the word "transsubstantiation" came into vogue. By 1150 the term was common in the works of the masters of theology of the University of Paris. Roland Bandinelli (later Pope Alexander III) used it in his *Book of Sentences* between 1140 and 1142. It passed into official documents of the Church and appeared in the profession of faith which the IVth Lateran Council directed against the Albigensians in 1215. Thus, it is not, as Luther claimed, the invention of St. Thomas Aquinas. Clumsy as the term may seem, it has the same basic significance as the statements of the true change and the true presence of Christ which earlier theologians had defended as the traditional faith of the Church. Thus, if one were to ask whether the Church has always professed faith in transsubstantiation, one would have to answer both affirmatively and negatively. The Church has always professed faith in the true change of bread and wine into the body and blood of Christ, but the Church has not always professed it in terms of transsubstantiation.

What is most important, however, is the shift in accent which took place in the theology of the Eucharist during the period between the 8th and the 13th century. Previous ages had experienced and understood the Eucharist as the celebration and daily nourishment of the unity of the community of the Church in the body of Christ. Medieval piety, on the other hand, considered the Eucharist as the possession of the priest and defined his priesthood in terms of the power to consecrate. And medieval theology placed its principal emphasis on the questions of the true (or in Scotus's term, "real") presence of Christ in the Eucharist and on the transsubstantiation which this true presence demands. The dimension of the sacramental meaning of this true presence and change was pushed aside and became quite marginal to the series of questions which constituted the theology of the Eucharist. Thus the shape of the devotion changed from the participation in Christ's sacrifice by the reception of the Sacred Host to the adoration of the Host and the "fruits" which this produced for the worshipper. Indeed, so rare was the reception of the Eucharist that the IVth Lateran Council was moved to introduce legislation to the effect that the faithful must confess and receive communion at least once a year under pain of being forbidden to enter the church and the denial of Christian burial (D 437). Some will insist that the entrance of Aristotle into western theology brought it to a peak. But at the same time, it should be clear that the Eucharistic life of the Church was a sad spectacle if it is compared with the meaning which is shown in its beginnings. "Take and eat . . ." and "Take and drink . . ." had become "Gaze on the Host and find your salvation in the gazing."

### *The Eucharist in the Reformation*

The opposition of the Reformation to the Eucharist took a twofold form: the argument over the real presence and the rejection of the sacrificial character of the Mass. Accordingly, the Council of Trent was called on to propose the faith of the Church in two sessions which adopted two decrees, one on the Eucharist (Session XIII, October, 1551) and another on the Sacrifice of the Mass (Session XXII, September, 1562). A third session treated of communion under both species (Session XXI, July, 1562). Whether this treatment of the Eucharist reflected current theological attitudes or whether the separate consideration of these three dimensions of the Eucharist are the result of this Tridentine statement is difficult to say, but the fact is that post-Tridentine theology treats the Eucharist according to the pattern of these decrees.

Luther's vituperations against the Mass might well shock the pious Catholic of today, but when one reads the list of abuses drawn up by the preparatory commission of the Council of Trent (August 8, 1562) one finds it easy to understand his disgust with the usages which surrounded the Eucharist in the 16th century. The commission's list is long enough, but some of the abuses listed are as follows: priests celebrating Mass so close together in the churches that their voices conflicted with one another; the celebration of other Masses during Solemn Mass; too many Masses being celebrated; Masses celebrated with no assistants whatever; no one, not even the ministers, receiving communion at Mass; the rivalry of processions of the Blessed Sacrament from different churches which break out into brawls; priests puffing and waving signs of the cross furiously over the Host and Chalice as if these signs contained the power of consecration; the elevation of the chalice by placing it on top of the head; the laying of "half-corrupt" cadavers on the altar during Mass; the congregation assisting with their dogs, falcons and hawks; visitors wandering through the choir during the choral offices chatting with monks and nuns, etc.[15] Of course, this list of abuses, even if the council had considered and implemented them, was too late to stop the fact of the Reformation. And, in any case, it was not simply the existence of such a sorry spectacle in the Eucharist which really led to the Reformation.

Apart from the particular reasons which the reformers had for rejecting the traditional teaching on the Eucharist, their rejection is basically an aspect of the threefold theological principle of the Reformation: man is saved by "Faith alone, Grace alone, Scripture alone." And the "alone" in this principle is a rejection of any intermediary in the salvation of the sinner, particularly the mediation of the earthly Church. Thus, the Reformation rejected the "works" of the Church in its insistence on "Faith alone," works

15. *Concilium Tridentinum. Diariorum, Actorum, Epistolarum Tractuum.* Nova Collectio. Ed. Görresgesellschaft. Freiburg, 1919. Vol. 8, p. 721. See Schmidt, *op. cit.*, p. 370.

which include the sacramental life of the Church primarily; it rejected preparation for salvation which comes from true repentance and conversion in its insistence on "Grace alone"; it rejected the traditions of the Church in its insistence on "Scripture alone." Thus, Luther insisted that trust in God was the unique principle of man's justification, adding his "alone" to Paul's citation of Habakkuk, "the righteous man shall live by his faith" (Rom. 1, 17; Hab. 2, 4).

This does not mean that Luther rejected the whole of the sacramental order. He retained Baptism, Confirmation and the Eucharist and originally retained the sacrament of Penance, although he later eliminated this latter. But even in these sacraments, Luther's insistence was still on "Faith alone." The sacraments were denied any objective mediating function in the insistence that it is only the faith of the believer which gives any power to the sacraments. Thus, the word of God must be preached in every sacramental action to arouse the faith of the believer, and the fruit of the sacramental action is the strengthening of the faith of the believer in the fact that he is justified, that his sins are no longer counted against him. Thus, in his theology of the Eucharist, Luther insisted that the purpose of the Eucharist is to stimulate the faith of the believer in the forgiveness of sins. He, in opposition to the Swiss and French reformers, insisted on the real presence of Christ in the Eucharist, but in his own way. For Luther, Christ is present only at the moment of the consecration, when the Passion is preached and commemorated, and at the moment of communion, when the death of the Lord is proclaimed and commemorated. The presence of Christ in the Eucharist does not endure beyond these moments. As for "transsubstantiation," Luther insisted that this was an invention of Aquinas without foundation in scripture or tradition.

Luther also rejected the teaching that the Mass is a sacrifice, beginning with attacks on the "fat bellies" who earned their living saying Mass in the chantries, but the theological basis for his rejection of the sacrificial character of the Mass is rather in the fact that this would place a human mediation between God and the sinner, an intolerable idea for Luther. Luther also reflects the current conviction that the Mass is the function of the priest alone in his insistence on communion under both Species. The reason for this insistence is Luther's teaching that since all believers are priests, all should communicate from the chalice, not merely the presiding minister of the Eucharist.

It is in the context of these problems, then, that the Council of Trent took up the question of the Eucharist in a well-balanced and comprehensive statement of the theology of the Eucharist. It is fashionable today to criticize and belittle the achievements of this council, but it should be stated that this was perhaps the most comprehensive conciliar statement in the history of the Church. It took twenty years and twenty-five sessions for the council to complete its work, and this it did in spite of the great opposition to its work from within the Church as well as from the political power of the era. The treatment of the Eucharist is scattered over three different sessions, separated by eleven years: Session XIII (November, 1551) producing the decree on the sacrament of the Eucharist, Session XXI (July, 1562) producing the decree on communion, and Session XXII (September, 1562). producing the decree on the sacrifice of the Mass. The importance of the decree on the Eucharist as well as the current discussion demand a more detailed analysis.

The *Decree on the Holy Eucharist* is composed of eight chapters, to which eleven canons are attached. Of these eight the first four merit close consideration. The first chapter treats of "The Real Presence of Our Lord Jesus Christ in the Most Holy Sacrament of the Eucharist." The chapter makes three dogmatic points. The first is the council's statement of the real presence of Christ in the Eucharist, "simply and openly" professing that our Lord Jesus Christ, true God and true man, is contained under the appearances of sensible realities after the consecration. The decree uses three adverbs to qualify this presence: truly, really and substantially. The text of this chapter does not elaborate on this threefold modification of Christ's presence, but the corresponding first canon opposes these adverbs to the positions of the reformers who rejected the real presence, opposing "truly, really and substantially" to "in a sign, in a figure or in the power" of Christ.

Thus, the statement is clearly directed against Zwingli and Hausenschein who maintained that Christ is only symbolically or figuratively present in the Eucharist and that the accounts of the institution of the Eucharist are to be interpreted symbolically and figuratively. It takes the position of Calvin into account when it adds the "substantially," rejecting Calvin's contention that the accounts of institution should be interpreted to mean that only the salvific power of Christ is present, not His true humanity and divinity.

The second point made in the first chapter is the fact that the presence of Christ is a *sacramental* presence, and in no way contradicts the fact that Christ can and does exist in His "natural manner of existence." The council insists that this type of presence cannot be described in human terms, but that it is possible for God. Finally, the third point is the statement that the basis of this belief is in the "proper and most obvious meaning" of the accounts of institution in the synoptic gospels and St. Paul.

The second chapter treats of the reason for the institution of the sacrament of the Eucharist. After stressing the reality of the presence of Christ's body and blood in the Eucharist, the council places this real presence once again in the context of the sacramental order. It is by the reception of this sacrament (i.e., in the act of communion) that Christ has commanded us to venerate His memory and to "announce His death until He comes" (1 Cor 11:26). The language of the council recalls St. Augustine's treatment of the real presence as a *sacrament,* for it speaks of the real presence of Christ as sacrament: "Moreover, He [Christ] wished this sacrament [His body and blood] to be received as the spiritual food of souls. . . ." It is because the believer receives the body and blood of Christ that he can live that life which Christ promised in the gospel of John: "He who eats me will live because of me" (Jn 6:58).

Thus, the council makes a clear and open statement of the real presence, but qualifies this statement with the consideration that this is a sacramental presence, not a real presence which has any human parallel. Further, the real body and blood of Christ is a sacrament, a sign of a still further meaning and power which

Christ's body and blood have for us: liberation from daily sins, preservation from mortal sin, the pledge of future glory and the symbol of the one body of Christ in which all are joined to the one Head in the bonds of one faith, hope and love.

The third chapter makes a strong point of the superiority of the Eucharist in the sacramental order. Granting that the Eucharist, like the other sacraments, is a sign (and using Berengar's definition, which it attributes to Augustine due to Gratian's attribution in the *Decretum*), the council states the superiority of the Eucharist in the fact that this sacramental sign contains the Author of Holiness not only in the actual use of the sacrament (communion), but also before the sacrament is received. The canon which corresponds to this statement enlarges this presence to a presence which is "before, in and after" communion, i.e., in the Sacred Species following the consecration and in the reserved Eucharist. This is directed against Luther's contention that Christ is only really present in the act of consecration and communion. The council answers by affirming the *abiding* presence of Christ in the Eucharist.

The second part of the chapter takes up the question of the manner in which Christ is present in the Eucharist, using the language which was the common possession of theology since the controversies with Berengar in the 11th century. The statement here is, from one point of view, a repetition of the teaching of the Council of Constance (1414–1418) in which the positions of John Wyclif and John Hus were condemned. Part of the purpose of Hus's teaching was to preserve the practice of communion under both species. In order to do this, he appealed to the words of consecration, —which clearly state that the body of Christ is present in the appearance of bread while the blood of Christ is present under the appearance of wine. Thus, in order to receive the whole Christ, one must receive communion under both species. This position is referred to as "dogmatic utraquism": the *dogmatic* statement that one must receive under both species (*sub utraque specie*) because of the meaning of the words of consecration. After the execution of Hus, this issue remained alive in Bohemia, and at the time of the Reformation the proponents of Hus's teaching and spirit found ready cause with the Reformation. Trent answers this position with the same language with which Alger of Liège and others answered it in the 13th century. Granted that by the force of the meaning of the words of consecration (*vi verborum*) the body of Christ is present under the species of bread and the blood of Christ is present under the species of wine, this is still the body and blood of the Risen Christ, and these cannot be separated from one another. Thus, because of the connection which the parts of Christ's humanity have in His Risen Humanity (*vi concomitantiae*) the whole humanity of Christ is present under each species and each part thereof, and because of the inseparable union of the divine and human in Christ in the hypostatic union, His divinity is also present under both species and each part of them. Thus, the whole Christ is entirely present under each species and in every part of each species.

In the fourth chapter, the council takes up Luther's contention that the expression "transsubstantiation" is an invention of Aquinas. The council does not answer Luther's position on historical grounds, though it well could have done this. It chose, rather, to answer him by simply stating that the Church itself has used the expression "transsubstantiation" as its own way of expressing the substantial change which takes place at the words of consecration in the Eucharist. It will be useful to present the whole of this chapter, which is short. If the translation seems over-literal, it is because the translation attempts to convey the ambiguity of certain elements of the chapter.

> Moreover, since Christ our Redeemer said that what he offered under the appearance of bread was truly His own body, it has always been the conviction in the Church of God, and this sacred synod also now declares again: that by the consecration of the bread and wine a change takes place of the whole substance of the bread into the substance of the body of Christ our Lord, and of the whole substance of the wine into the substance of His blood. And this conversion has suitably and properly been called transsubstantiation by the holy catholic Church.

The council also framed the following canon as a sanction to the teaching of the decree:

If anyone says that in the most holy sacrament of the Eucharist the substance of bread and wine remain together with the body and blood of Christ, or if anyone denies that wonderful and unique change of the whole substance of bread into the body and of the whole substance of the wine into the blood, while the appearances of bread and wine remain, a change which the Church most suitably calls "transsubstantiation," let him be anathema. [Canon 2]

The chapter and canon, then, make three affirmations. First, the Council affirms the true change which takes place in the consecration. But this change presupposes what the council prefaces to the affirmation of the true change: the real presence of Christ in the gift of the Eucharist. And finally, the third affirmation: that of the name of the change. The council states that the Church has called this change transsubstantiation "suitably and properly" (*convenienter et proprie*) and "most suitably" (*aptissime*). Thus, although the truth of the change in the consecration is stated as the constant conviction of the Church and reaffirmed in this decree, the basis for the Church's faith in this change is not any independent concern for the bare physical fact of the change. The basis for the Church's faith in this change is the Church's faith in the true presence of Christ's humanity and divinity in the sacrament under the manifestation of bread and wine.

The work of the theological commissions in the preparation of this decree and the discussion of it on the floor of the council show the intimate relationship between the statement of the real presence and the statement of the true change of bread and wine into the body and blood of Christ. Some wanted to accommodate Luther to the extent of eliminating the expression "transsubstantiation" completely from the decree. They preferred that the chapter and canon read: "If anyone states that the body and blood of Christ are present in the Eucharist in a manner other than that which the Church has always held . . ."[16] But to these men it was pointed out that there was no reason for fearing the expression. The language of the Church's expression of her faith grows with each age,

16. *Op. cit.,* vol. 6, pp. 160–161.

as is shown by the use of the expression "consubstantial" (*homoousios*) used to describe the unity of Father and Son in the Arian controversies of the 4th and 5th centuries. This is not biblical language, but it is the language of the Church and it has served as the shibboleth of orthodox faith in the Trinity. And the term "transsubstantiation," granted its non-biblical character, can well serve the same purpose. Basically, it is simply the statement of the Church's faith in the Eucharist in the peculiar circumstances of the Reformation.

Others objected to the canon on transsubstantiation precisely because it is simply a statement of the Church's faith in the real presence of Christ in the Eucharist, and that therefore it was reductively a repetition of the first canon of the decree, which states the real presence of Christ. It added nothing new to the decree. To these men it was pointed out that the times demanded an affirmation of the legitimacy of the Church's theological and doctrinal traditions in the face of the "Scripture alone" of the Reformation. Further, the theologians and council Fathers firmly rejected the opinion of some theologians who insisted that the Church came to her faith in the real presence of Christ through her teaching on transsubstantiation! The council insisted that exactly the opposite is the case: the Church comes to her statement of true change (called transsubstantiation) through her biblical faith in the truth of Christ's words: "This is my body," "This is my blood."

There is a third level on which these statements of the decree can be discussed, and this is the level of the philosophical thought-forms which the expression "transsubstantiation" brings to mind. It is heard often enough that the Council of Trent purposely removed itself from any Aristotelian understanding of "substantial change" and "substance." This seems to be an oversimplification. It is true that the correlative expression for "substance" is "appearances" not "accidents" in the decree. But this does not seem to be a complete rejection of Aristotelian thought-forms in itself. There is no such purpose expressed in the discussions of the commissions or the discussions on the floor of the council. Indeed, one proposal for the canon on transsubstantiation did use the expression "accidents" instead of "appearances" and in the discussion of this version, the Fathers simply voted that either formulation was acceptable (*"Utraque lectio placet"*). This reaction is to be expected from men of the 16th century. They were men of their time, with very particular and concrete backgrounds. To expect them to divorce themselves from the Aristotelian framework of natural philosophy is tantamount to expecting them to think and act in a complete vacuum. It is true that their primary purpose in the council is the affirmation of biblical faith in the Eucharist, but the only terms in which men of their time could have expressed this faith and the reality of the change which takes place in the Eucharist were the terms of the schools of the time: the Aristotelian categories of substance and accidents, expressing the basic distinction between the reality and the appearance and action of that reality on other realities.

Thus, the essential affirmations of this decree on the Eucharist can be reduced to two: the biblical faith of the Church in the real sacramental presence of Christ in the Eucharist, and the change of the bread and wine into the body and blood of Christ which this real presence demands. The term "transsubstantiation" is proposed by the council in the sense that this is suitable and proper for the expression of this basic biblical faith, —this, at least in the sense that it is not unsuitable and improper as the Reformation theologians would have it. This is the faith of Trent. It is not the beginning nor is it the end of the Church's dogmatic and theological traditions; indeed, the fact that it is only one moment of that tradition is illustrated quite clearly by its adoption of the word "transsubstantiation" as a shibboleth of orthodox belief. This does not mean that those who did not express their faith in this way were unorthodox. Quite to the contrary, the Church expressed her faith with complete satisfaction for over a thousand years without this expression. But the adoption of the term expresses the Church's confidence in dogmatic and theological tradition in the face of their rejection by the Reformation. It is a shibboleth in this last sense.

Eleven years after the decree on the Holy Eucharist, the council took up the questions of communion and the sacrifice of the Mass. One would like to see a strong statement on the necessity of sacramental communion, but in the context of the Reformation this is too much to expect. It must be kept in mind that the paradigm of Eucharistic piety of the 16th century, the Mass at which the faithful assisted without communicating sacramentally, was under attack and consequently to be defended by the council. Further, it should be remembered that this was an era in which communion was not encouraged, the desires of the council notwithstanding. Even in the cloister, communion was only permitted at stated, and this not frequent, intervals with the advice and consent of one's confessor. The lives of the saints from this time relate of the intense preparation for communion which lasted for days and weeks.

The council's decree on communion is not a document for the edification of the faithful. Rather it is a defensive apology for the practice of communion under one species, that of bread. Though the council probably had Luther in mind in this decree, the language of the document seems rather to refer to the petition of the Duke of Bavaria[17] and to the problems of the Slavic countries still under the remote influence of John Hus, where the demand for the chalice was still a point of national honor. The third chapter of the decree, which states that the whole Christ is present under each species, seems to be directed against the battle cry of the Calixtines of Poland, "*Calix caro conjunx*" (chalice [for the laity], meat [on Friday], wife [for the clergy]). The Reformation made this its own battle cry.

The *Decree on the Most Holy Sacrifice of the Mass* has the same apologetic tone. The first chapter presents a well-balanced statement on the connection between the real presence, communion and the sacrifice. The description of the Last Supper places the sacrificial character of the Eucharist in the fact that Jesus gave His body and blood to His disciples to eat and drink under the appearances of bread and wine. His command "Do this in commemoration of me" is the gift of the Eucharist and, at the same time, the constitution of a new priesthood and of an eternal

17. *Op. cit.*, vol. 8, pp. 528 ff.

sacrifice. The celebration of the old Passover leads to the gift of a new Passover which is the commemoration of man's redemption in Jesus' return to the Father. Here is an integrated statement of the fact that it is in eating and drinking that Christ's sacrifice is renewed and commemorated sacramentally and the fruits of that sacrifice are granted to the believer.

But apart from this general statement of the faith of the Church, the rest of the decree is devoted to a defense of the propitiatory character of the Mass, the canon, Masses in honor of the saints, the ceremonies of the Solemn Mass, Latin as the language of the liturgy, and the Mass at which no one except the celebrant communicates. Regarding this last, the Mass at which no one communicates except the celebrant, the council does express a velleity (the council would wish: *optaret*) that the faithful communicate at every Mass, a courageous statement in the face of the general attitude toward communion in the Church, but even this mild statement is weakened by the further statement that the council approves and commends the Masses in which no one except the celebrant communicates. The council states that these are not private Masses but are truly public (*vere communes*) because the faithful participate spiritually and because they are celebrated on behalf of the entire Church.

The effect of the Council of Trent on the life of the Church was deep and longlasting. Its insistence on the education of the clergy was perhaps its greatest accomplishment. But in the area of the Eucharistic piety of the Church, its effect was far from a renewal. What it accomplished was rather the hardening of the piety of the time. The Council itself became the textbook for the education of clergy and laity alike, and in the area of the theology of the Eucharist, the council's disparate emphasis on real presence, communion and the sacrifice of the Mass as three rather unrelated values in the Eucharist set the tone for the theology of the Eucharist and Eucharistic piety for several centuries. The theology of the Eucharist centers around the question of the real presence. Eucharistic piety centers around the tabernacle and the procession of the Blessed Sacrament. The sacrifice of the Mass becomes the Sunday obligation, generally disassociated from Eucharistic piety except for the elevation of the Host. If there is any furthering of theology in the area of the Eucharist, it is only to be found in the many theoretical attempts to explain the reason why the Eucharist is a sacrifice. Whatever one thinks of the value of this speculation today, the fact is that it served to isolate the sacrificial character of the Eucharist even more from the specifically sacramental theology of the Eucharist. One is not surprised to hear from priests who have been trained in this tradition the firm conviction that the Mass is not a sacrament, that it is sacrifice and that only.

### *Renewal in Eucharistic Theology*

The beginnings of renewal in Eucharistic theology cannot be limited to any one phenomenon in the life of the Church. Many influences conspired to bring about the present efforts at renewal. It would seem, however, that one of the earliest and most crucial turning points was the work of the Catholic theological faculty at Tübingen in the first decades of the 19th century. What made this faculty such a critical factor in the history of theology was the fact that its work constituted a sharp break with the spirit and forms of post-Tridentine theology. While theologians generally devoted their efforts either to the polemic defence of the teaching of Trent or to intra-mural Catholic questions, the Tübingen faculty began to place a strong emphasis on the communitarian life of the Church and on the critical study of the sources of the Church's traditions.

At the same time, the foundations for the revival of the purer forms of liturgical worship among the Benedictines began with the work of Dom Prosper Guéranger. His studies on the Church's liturgical year and his *Liturgical Institutions* began to reëmphasize the official prayer of the Church and its preëminence over private devotions. It may be true that his studies were academic and the cultivation of the monastic liturgy and of Gregorian Chant are far from what is considered renewal today. But the work of Dom Guéranger and his successors did create a new experience of Eucharistic worship. And although this experience was not aimed at the mass of Catholics, the experience of the liturgy at Solesmes was a beginning for those who shared in it. It was these retreatants and scholars who carried the word of renewal beyond the confines of Solesmes. Thus the monks of Solesmes, together with the scholars of Tübingen, were preparing the theological and liturgical ground for a deeper and richer appreciation of the Church's Eucharistic worship.

Early in the 20th century, Pope Pius X added great impetus to the movement by his decrees on participation in the Eucharist and on the desirability of frequent, even daily, communion. The decree on frequent communion gave impetus to a movement in the Church which began to reunite the fragmented experience of the Eucharist which was so common in the Church since the 12th century. The decree on sacred music, it is true, proposed what would seem to the present day to be an unrealistic ideal, the image of hundreds and thousands of the faithful chanting the Gregorian chants at Mass with some proficiency. In spite of many efforts, the movement never really took hold on any large scale. But these decrees did constitute a sharp change of direction in the prevalent attitudes toward the Eucharist.

The Benedictine efforts at the purification of and a greater participation in the liturgy continued with the work of Dom Lambert Beauduin in Belgium, and especially with that of the great abbot of Maria Laach, Abbot Ildefons Herwegen. The great abbeys of Europe, Solesmes; Maredsous, with the biblical and liturgical spirituality of Dom Columba Marmion; Beuron, with its attempts at the purification and refinement of liturgical art; and Maria Laach with its center for scientific liturgical studies, all contributed greatly to the formation of an educated laity who continued to work for liturgical reform in their own countries. From these beginnings grew the various national liturgical days and weeks which stimulated interest in and conveyed an experience of the Eucharist which was far more universal than previously. And the interest which was stimulated was not simply an aesthetic interest in the purity of the Roman liturgy and Gregorian chant. The liturgical institutes were also, especially in Belgium, associated with the Catholic Action groups. The experience of the Eucharist was meant to be an explicit proclamation of faith in a deep experience of Christian unity, and, at the same time, the liturgical experience was aimed at a deeper living of the Christian life from day to day.

Of course, this work did not proceed smoothly. Opposition accompanied it from the start. Theologians of a more traditionalist cast opposed the "exaggerations" of the new scientific study of the liturgy and of the liturgical movement itself. Mass celebrated facing the congregation, the suppression of the recitation of the rosary during Mass, the removal of the tabernacle from the altar, the dialogue form of celebrating the Eucharist, these and other attempts at reform were condemned by bishops almost from the start. In 1947, Pius XII published his monumental letter on the liturgy, *Mediator Dei,* stressing the value and necessity of participation in the Eucharist, the act of communion as the completion of participation in the sacrifice of the Mass, the calling of all Christians to a priestly worship of God in Christ. But even in this excellent letter, the Pope felt bound to stress opposite values, the fact that the faithful are not priests in the same way that the clergy are, the fact that liturgical piety is no substitute for personal piety, the fact that communion of the faithful is not absolutely necessary for the "completion of the sacrifice" of the Mass. And the Pope's concern was not without foundation. Voices were being raised in favor of a vernacular liturgy, communion under both species, concelebration and similar liturgical forms which were shocking to the hierarchy as late as 1945. At that time, Msgr. Romano Guardini had to write to the Bishop of Mainz explaining that these demands were not the hallmark of the liturgical movement. However, these crises in the history of the movement had a positive effect in the fact that the bishops of the Fulda Union erected a liturgical commission for Germany which regulated the progress of the liturgical reform. This gave status to the movement as well as affording it the protection of the German hierarchy. The establishment of the German liturgical commission was soon followed by the establishment of commissions in Austria, and eventually in France and Holland. And the worth of the work of these commissions became evident in the fact that the reformation of the liturgical life of the Church has largely followed the patterns of worship adopted in the rituals of Germany and Austria.

The liturgical movement has been accompanied almost from its start by a renewed interest in a broader theological study of the Eucharist. The work of the Tübingen faculty has produced studies, such as those of Karl Adam and Matthias Joseph Scheeben, in which the theology of the incarnation, the Church and the sacraments are deepened by the study of these mysteries in the light of one another. The description of Christ as "primal sacrament" (*Ursakrament*) has deepened both the theology of the incarnation (and Church) and the theology of the sacraments. The strong orientation toward the study of the living Church as a community in Christ which characterized this school from the beginning has had a profound influence on European theology. It has focused attention once again on the fact that the Eucharist is the sacrament of the Church as a community.

Further, ecumenical studies have tended to abandon the polemical concentration of the theology of the Eucharist on the questions of the real presence and the sacrifice of the Mass and introduced a new unity into the theology of the Eucharist. With the ecumenical concentration on what is common to all Christian belief, there has been a renewed interest in the Eucharist as a sacrament which, while it does not depend for its reality on human faith, demands nonetheless the faith and devotion of the believer for its full effectiveness.

The change in thought-forms in the contemporary European view of human existence and its experience has also prompted renewed interest in every aspect of theology in the effort to restate the belief of the Church in terms which interest and appeal to men of this day and age. Readers of the documents of the Second Vatican Council will be interested, as theologians of today have been interested, in the remarkable change in the formulation of Catholic teaching. They will notice the change to a more biblical and personal style in the decrees which speak of almost every aspect of the life of the Church. But these documents cannot be read as if they have sprung full-grown out of a historical vacuum. The reason for their change of style is the change in the life of the Church and the change in the style of theology which has been characteristic of almost the past hundred years. This change has not always been carried on in peace and tranquillity. There has been suspicion, fear; there have been condemnations. But slowly the change has come, and, hopefully, the change will continue.

The work of renewal in the theology of the Eucharist, as in every aspect of theology today, can hardly be called a task completed. But one can well ask whether it will ever be so. The mystery of faith and the mystery of the Eucharist always have and always will escape any efforts to control them by categories of human thought and experience. This is a task which has come to be seen as the on-going task of theology; this is the true *theologia perennis,* the continual questioning and restatement of the biblical faith of the Church. The door is not closed to such a task. In spite of the difficulties and dangers it always presents, the serious theologian will always find the way open for the serious work of grasping at the heart of belief and stating it forthrightly to the men of every age and every place.

CHAPTER TWO

# THE BIBLICAL FAITH

## *The Institution of the Eucharist*

THEOLOGICALLY, the reality of what takes place in the celebration of the Eucharist is intimately bound to the events of the Last Supper, in which the Church has always seen the "institution" of the Eucharist. Because of the influence of hylomorphism, however, theologians have generally tended to think of the institution of the sacraments in general and of the Eucharist in particular as a matter of the determination, in some way, of the "matter" and "form" of the sacraments by Christ. These have been considered to be the component elements in the "essence" of the sacrament. In an Aristotelian style of thought, this analysis does say something, provided that this sacramental use of hylomorphism is always qualified by the consideration that the sacrament is not simply the external ritual, but is, rather, the visible ritual as a *sign-action.* And from this point of view, "matter" and "form" in the sacraments can be used in their Aristotelian sense of their being correlative aspects in the constitution of the sign-act: its *capacity* to express sacramental meaning ("matter") and the *actual determination* of the sacramental meaning in the ritual ("form"). This means that the institution of the sacrament is not so much a matter of the determination of the elements of the ritual itself (the words and actions as matter and form) as the determination of the sacramental meaning and of the religious sign-action which has an objective capacity to contain the sacramental meaning.

All too often this question of the institution of the sacraments has been divorced from the concrete historical way in which God has brought about the dispensation of salvation. In the face of the Reformation, of course, the theological treatment of this question was conditioned by the rejection of some of the sacraments by the reformers. The answer of the Catholic theologians was to attempt to demonstrate that these sacraments, indeed in some cases the ritual itself, can be traced back to Christ's own determination. Later centuries modified this extreme position in a variety of opinions as to how Christ did institute the sacraments. But almost all of these treatments still have in common the attempt to justify the ritual, while they generally ignore the fact that this ritual is a sign. Contemporary treatments of the sacraments are changing the perspective of this question, finding the heart of the reality ("essence of the sacrament") in the sacramental meaning as this is incarnate in the ritual. They are also placing the Christian sacramental dispensation in a more explicit continuity with the sacramental religion of Israel. Scripture scholars (Catholic and Protestant alike) have contributed greatly to this work, pointing out that the religious ritual which is central to all sacramental action in the Church today was already in existence, with its own religious meaning and power, at the time of the life of Jesus.

Thus, for example, it is evident to any reader of the New Testament that the ritual of Baptism for the remission of sins as a sign of the incorporation into a community was already in existence at the time of Jesus. He Himself was baptized by John (Mt 13:11–17 and parallels). The cultic confession of sin and repentance was a part of the ritual of Israel from the very beginnings of Solomon's temple (1 Kgs 8:22 ff.). The anointing of the sick as the sign of the presence of God's power against evil was attested by rabbinic sources.[1] Marriage, of course, is a deeply secular reality which was always a strictly family affair only gradually taking on the form of religious celebration in Christianity until the Council of Trent passed universal legislation

1. H. Strack, and P. Billerbeck, *Kommentar zum Neuen Testament aus Talmud und Midrash.* Munich, 1961 (3rd ed.), vol. II, pp. 11–12.

requiring the presence of a priest and other witnesses for the validity of the marriage. But even this legislation does not make the priest the minister of the sacrament. There is after all, no essential *religious* ritual which constitutes marriage as a sacrament. However, the very first pages of Genesis (2:18 ff.) attest to the conviction of the existence of a religious meaning and value in marriage from the beginning, a meaning which Christ Himself later reaffirmed (Mt 19:4 ff.). And for this reason, the community of Israel, like the Church today, watched carefully over the married life of its members.

Thus, the institution of the sacraments does not appear so much to be a matter of the determination of a ritual of actions and words as it is a matter of the transformation of the inner meaning and value of these actions by the creative word of Christ. His life and death, the historical shape of God's ultimate redemptive act, become the central content of this ritual. It is Christ and the saving favor which God manifests and grants in and through Him which is now the central religious meaning and power of the *Christian* sacraments.

The answer to the question of how Christ transformed the meaning and power of the religious ritual of Israel is not always a matter of record in the scriptures. Some theologians appeal to the period following the resurrection of Christ as the time when the sacraments were instituted, this in terms of a specific meaning being assigned to a specific rite. Whatever the value of this position may be, it should be pointed out that there is a profound transformation in the whole life of Israel brought about by God in the very reality of the life of Christ. For it is the historical reality of the life and death of Jesus, with the religious meaning and power incarnate in Him, which is the ultimate direction woven into the life of Israel as a people.

It is basically God's revelation of himself to the tribes enslaved in Israel which originally gathered these tribes together into a people, giving their existence a unity hitherto unknown. And the root of this unity is to be found in the fact that the very self-identity of these tribes as a people derived from the personal revelation of Yahweh as their God. In the light of historical studies, it would not seem that this personal revelation of itself immediately and radically changed the life of this people, at least in its outward forms. What was radically changed was the *inner meaning* of the life of the people as such. Centuries of reflection on the central meaning of their life as a people (viz., on the fact that Yahweh is *their* God and that they are *His* people) gradually transformed the consciousness of Israel into the shape which is presented in the biblical sources. And the image which is presented is that of a people constantly under the guidance of their God. Their history, their temple cult, the very structure of the temple itself are presented as divinely revealed and divinely created institutions. And this religious conviction reflects the basic theological insight of the biblical authors into the shape of Israel's life history: the fact that Israel's life as a people and the cultic forms in which she expressed that life were all the gift of their God. But this does not necessarily mean that the concrete forms of temple worship and the laws which governed Israel's life were all the result of specific divine revelations. It seems far more in keeping with historical fact that Israel gradually refined and transformed her own nomadic origins under the impetus of religious reflection on the absolutely unique value which her faith found at the center of her life as a people: the fact that she is God's people. True, her life and her worship are God's gift, but the concrete historical forms of her life and worship are also the result of centuries of historical evolution in that process of purification and refinement of religious consciousness which rose out of the religious reflection on her unique identity as a people. Thus, the basic transformation which takes place in the original constitution of Israel as a people is given in the fact that God revealed Himself personally to Israel as Yahweh, and claimed this people as His own. It is this revelation, woven into the whole life of this particular group of tribes, which transforms the whole meaning and value of her earthly and human reality.

However, woven into the pattern of the historical existence of the people there is also a direction toward Christ. The great historical stimulus for the consciousness of this eschatological dimension in the life of Israel was, of course, the experience of defeat and destruction which accompanied the fall of Israel in the 7th century BC. This experience brought to the consciousness of Israel an awareness of the restoration which God would accomplish in a new Temple, a new David, the "anointed one," the "righteous one" who is the promise of the Servant Songs of Deutero-Isaiah. Whatever is to be said of the identity of the Servant in the mind of the authors of Deutero-Isaiah, the fulfillment of this promise is concretely brought about by God in the Incarnation in which the new Israel comes into history in Christ. In this sense, then, the very historical reality of the life and death of Christ interiorly transforms the meaning of Israel's life. The fulfillment of her historical existence is in Him personally, in Emmanuel, God who dwells with man. It is in this framework that the basic transformation of the meaning and power of Israel's ritual religion takes place.

Thus, the baptism which incorporated the convert into the people of Israel, is now to be a Baptism into the people whom God has gathered together in Christ (Rom 6:4–11). And this initiation is now completed with the expectation of Israel: the Spirit of righteousness whose outpouring is the sign of the last days (Acts 2:38). The judgment which calls men to repentance is no longer the "death" of Genesis 2:17. Now it is the judgment of life which calls men to repent and the life given is the life of the Risen One (Jn 20:22–23). The power of God against sickness is revealed now in the "name of the Lord of glory, Jesus Christ" (Jas 5:14–15; 2:1). The religious meaning and power incarnate in the love of husband and wife finds the fulfillment of the meaning which it had from the beginning in the love of Christ for the Church (Eph 5:31–32).

However implicit this sacramental principle may be for the other sacraments, it is most explicit in the New Testament image of the meaning of the Eucharist. Both the accounts of the institution of the Eucharist in the synoptic gospels and in St. Paul, and John's theology of the meaning and reality of the Eucharist, set Christ's action quite explicitly in a paschal context. Whether this means that the institution of the Eucharist took place historically in the actual celebration of the paschal supper by Jesus and His disciples is not at issue here. What is at issue is the fact that the New Testament does present the Eucharist as a fulfillment of the meaning and power which was incarnate in the paschal celebration. Thus, before the character of the change is taken up, the question of the meaning of Passover itself should be clarified. It would seem that a certain lack of clarity in this respect is at the bottom of the two hard positions today with regard to the question whether the Mass is a banquet or a sacrifice.

The celebration of Passover at the time of Christ was actually the celebration of two feasts which were originally distinct from one another: *pesaḥ* (Passover) and *maṣṣôth* (Unleavened Bread). The two feasts had approximately the same meaning but they came from two different situations. Passover came from the religion of the nomadic shepherds. It was the sacrifice of a young animal offered to insure the increase and well-being of the flocks. Roland de Vaux suggests that it was offered at the time of the departure of the shepherd tribes for their spring pasture. The blood of the slain animal was sprinkled on the tent-poles to insure the safety of the tribe itself.[2] The Feast of Unleavened Bread, on the other hand, was the spring celebration of the sedentary farmer. It marked the beginning of the barley harvest, and during the first seven days of this harvest only the newly harvested grain was eaten in an unleavened bread made without the ferment which remained from the previous year's grain. Thus, it marked the beginning of the new season, and this grain was offered to the god for the same reason that the young animal was killed at Passover: in thanksgiving for the harvest and as a sacrifice to insure the fertility of the soil and the unity of the people. De Vaux suggests that this feast was not kept in Israel until after the settlement in Canaan.[3] In their final fusion, however, Unleavened Bread was observed as the octave of Passover, the latter being celebrated on the 14th of Nisan, the former from the 15th to the 21st of Nisan. Thus Unleavened Bread and Passover both constituted the cultic memorial and celebration of

2. *Ancient Israel. Its Life and Institutions,* New York and London, 1961, p. 489.

3. *Op. cit.,* pp. 490–491.

the momentous event of the Exodus. This is the eventual character which the biblical sources gave to the feasts (Deut 16:1–8).

There was also an evolution in the very shape of the celebration of the feasts. Exodus 12 gives the celebration the character of a family feast whose meaning is the strengthening of the tribal bond. The year-old lamb was slain publicly by the father of the family, eaten ritually in the home while the father explained the commemorative meaning of this action. By the time of the Deuteronomic reform (7th century BC), however, the slaying of the lamb and the ritual meal was removed from the market place and the home to the temple (2 Kgs 23:21; 2 Chron 34:29—35:19). The familial character of the feasts was lost and it became instead the feast of the people. The Levites became the ones who slaughtered the lambs, and in place of sprinkling blood on the doorposts, the blood was poured out by priests at the foot of the altar of sacrifice in the temple. But this national character of the feast was already present in the familial celebrations in the prescriptions that non-Israelites cannot participate in this feast until they are circumcised (Num 9:14), and that those who were unclean were still bound to celebrate the feast under the pain of excommunication (9:13).

By the time of Christ, however, the enormous numbers of pilgrims who came to the temple for the Passover precluded the possibility of their eating the paschal meal in the temple. Accordingly, the eating of the paschal meal was transferred to the homes of Jerusalem and the huge camps which surrounded the city.

Within this evolution, nevertheless, there remained a unity of meaning and power in the unity between the table and the altar. St. Paul reflected this understanding when he asked the Corinthians to "Consider the practice of Israel; are not those who eat the sacrifices communicants in the altar of sacrifice?" (1 Cor 10:18). At its heart, the eating of the paschal meal was that of a sacramental communion in the temple sacrifice of the paschal lamb. This was a communion-sacrifice in which those who ate were joyfully sharing in the act of worship performed in the sacrificial slaying of the lamb. Thus, the altar and the table were not disparate or contradictory elements on the observance of Pasch, but were rather two moments of one sacramental act whose meaning bound them together. The eating of the paschal lamb was the sacramental communion in the sacramental meaning of the sacrifice: the renewal in Israel of the religious event of the Exodus. In this act (sacrifice and eating of the sacrifice) the unity of the people was created by God as He shared the sacrifice with His people. Israel was once again released from the slavery of all that Egypt meant to her. Israel joyfully renewed her covenant with God and was made to be (once again, *in* this act) the people of God. Altar and table were bound into a sacramental unity by the central religious significance of the sacrifice of the paschal lamb.

Further, the shape of the paschal meal itself was calculated to do far more than merely recall the fact that the Exodus took place. Every liturgical detail was meant to make Israel relive the Exodus. The dress was that of a people on the move, sandals, staffs, clothing bound up for the journey through the desert. The food itself suggested the same experience: the unleavened bread, baked in haste because of the emergency of the moment, the bitter herbs which are the greens of the desert, the lamb cooked without butchering, eaten in haste. All of this, liturgical as it was, recreated the experience of the Exodus in the very act of its celebration. Far more evocative and creative of the religious meaning of this liturgical meal, however, were the words of the father as he explained the meaning of the meal and blessed God for its meaning and power. The meal opened with the blessing of the feast in which the father blessed God for giving this feast to His people. After bitter herbs were dipped into a bowl of sauce, the meal was served. But before the eating, the father carefully explained the meaning of this meal. The bread is the bread of affliction and haste which evokes the years in the desert; the lamb evokes the night of deliverance from Egypt. Then the father said a blessing before breaking the bread and giving it to the family. He blessed God for the food which was before the family and for what it meant. After the bread was passed, the lamb was eaten. And at the end of the meal, the father took a cup of wine and said a final blessing, praising God for the plenty of the earth, the land in which Israel dwelt, and prayed for God's mercy and protection on His people Israel, on His city Jerusalem, on the dwelling place of His glory on Zion, and finally on the temple which was the center of true worship. He concluded with a final blessing: "Blessed art thou, O Lord, who buildest Jerusalem."[4] Pierre Benoit points out that these blessings are not simply recollections of the past benefits of God. They confer on the meal itself a power to evoke the past and hope for the future in such a way that those who ate relived in a real way the trials of the exodus and came thence to live in the hope of the messianic promises.[5] The Passover meal, then, with its intimate link with the sacrificial slaying of the paschal lamb, was a commemoration of Exodus, to be sure, but it was a commemoration in celebration. It celebrated the gracious favor of God who did wonderful things for Israel in the past. But it did not celebrate a past or absent God. It celebrated Israel's God who gave the Exodus, the feast, the food and the grace of being His people in the act of the yearly celebration itself.

It is against this background that some appreciation can be gained of the meaning and power of the action of Christ in His celebration of Passover in the Last Supper. In setting the institution of the Eucharist into the context of the paschal meal, the New Testament authors related the actions of Jesus to the moments of the ceremonial meal. The departure of the betrayer followed the initial ceremony of dipping into the bitter herbs (Mt 26:20–25). The recitation of the *haggadah* while the paschal meal itself was lying on the table before them afforded a suitable opportunity for Jesus to explain the meaning of the Unleavened Bread and the Lamb in terms of His own act of deliverance. The meaning and power of this meal was creatively

4. J. Jeremias, *The Eucharistic Words of Jesus,* New York and London, 1966, p. 110. See also P. Benoit, O.P., "The Accounts of Institution and What They Mean," in *The Eucharist in the New Testament. A Symposium.* Edited by J. Delorme. Baltimore and Dublin, 1964, pp. 73–75.

5. "Eucharistie," in *Vocabulaire de Théologie Biblique.* Edited by X. Léon-Dufour. Paris, 1962, p. 329.

evoked by the creative word of Jesus. The passing of the cup which concluded this part of the meal was accompanied by Jesus' announcement that, much as He wished it, he would not eat of this supper until it was fulfilled in the kingdom of God (Lk 22:15–18). Then He began the meal proper with the blessing traditionally spoken at the breaking of the Unleavened Bread. Usually, the bread was passed from hand to hand in silence, everyone waiting for the head of the house to begin eating. But in this meal, the traditional silence was broken. As the bread passed from hand to hand, the voice of Jesus broke in: "Take and eat. This is my body." And after all had eaten the paschal lamb, Jesus took up the final cup, the "cup of benediction." The meal was about to be ended. After saying the traditional blessing, Jesus gave this cup to His disciples and said, "Drink this, this is my 'covenant blood.'"

Jesus, then, was giving His own body and blood to His disciples. But this was not simply a gift. Their eating and drinking was a communion in a sacrifice which was present before them in the person of Jesus. Paul, (1 Cor 11:24), Luke (22:19) and John (6:51) qualify the meaning of "This is my body" with the addition of "for you," "given for you," and "for the life of the world." Matthew and Mark include this same sacrificial qualification in the words spoken over the final cup: "This is my covenant blood, poured out for you" (Mk 14:42) and "poured out for the forgiveness of sins" (Mt 26:27–28).

Something of capital importance emerges from this paschal setting. It is the fact that the transformation which takes place is not simply the transformation of a piece of bread. It is rather the transformation of the religious meaning and power of the *unleavened bread eaten in the paschal meal.* It is the transformation of the sacrificial meaning and power of the Unleavened Bread. Rather than evoking the reality of the sacrifice of the paschal lamb in the unity of the paschal table with the altar in the temple, eating of this Bread now evokes the reality of a sacrifice which is timelessly present in the person of Jesus. Drinking from this cup now means and is participation in the new covenant which God has given to man in Jesus. It means the constantly renewed gift of belonging to that people whom God has created in Jesus.

## *The Presence of Christ*

The presence of Christ in the Eucharist, indeed the *real* presence of Christ, is a clear datum of the scriptural accounts of the institution of the Eucharist. However, as tautological as Carlstadt's position may seem to Catholic theologians (viz., Jesus pointed to Himself when He said, "This is my body"), the issue which it raises is an important one. It is the problem of the relation of the Last Supper to the daily celebration of the Eucharist in the Church. If the New Testament accounts are taken as "history" in a somewhat fundamentalist sense, the objection could be posed that, granted the real bodily presence of Christ at the Last Supper, this has nothing to say about the real presence of Christ in the Eucharist. An appeal could be made, in reply, to the words of Jesus, "Do this for my remembrance" (1 Cor 11:25). But it could then be pointed out that this saying is only given clearly in St. Paul's account, an account, moreover, of one who was not there. Further, Paul's disciple, Luke, may or may not report this saying, and the accounts of Matthew and Mark (men who were probably present) definitely omit it. One can see that this type of reply misses the real issue, not so much because it fails to count heads properly, but rather because it accepts the state of the question which permits the difficulty to rise in the first place. The real answer is to be found in the determination of what the gospel is really saying. And this raises the question of the gospels as history. A full treatment of this problem is not possible here, but some pertinent facts can be indicated which will contribute to an understanding of the question of the presence of Christ in the Eucharist.

Since the Modernist crisis in the beginning of the present century, the Church has seen the need time and again of insisting on the genuinely historical character of the scriptures in general and of the New Testament in particular. The reasons for this insistence have varied with the times and one still finds an echo of this concern in the *Dogmatic Constitution on Divine Revelation* of the Second Vatican Council.[6] There is a strong insistence in the constitution on the fact that the gospels faithfully hand on what Jesus said and did in His earthly life and that, while the authors condense, synthesize and interpret the life of Jesus, they still tell us what He really did and said. And anyone who is familiar with the more existential styles of exegesis today will see the importance of such a statement. Without it, the gospels are easily emptied of any real content. However, the council, reflecting the findings of contemporary biblical studies, does state that the evangelists did report the life of Jesus from a particular point of view, condensing, synthesizing, interpreting His life. And the reason for this is the fact that, while the evangelists did hand on what really happened, their interpretation of what happened is centered around the heart of the gospels, the preaching of the "good news" that God has saved man in Christ. This means that the gospels are not historical in the sense that the histories of Josephus and Pliny are histories. The gospels narrate the life of Jesus in such a way that the Christian community will find the meaning of its own life in the life of Jesus.

This principle of interpretation is seen particularly clearly in the accounts of the Last Supper in the gospels and in St. Paul. It is present in St. John's treatment of the Eucharist in the discourse on the Bread of Life (6:35–71). If John's treatment is set into the context of its historical origins, there emerges a dimension of meaning which constitutes a strongly apologetic statement of the real presence. The Jews argue among themselves, "How can this man give us His flesh to eat?" (6:52). Their confusion, being outsiders, can well be understood. But even some of His own disciples murmur against Jesus because this is a "hard saying" and take offense against it (6:60–62). Jesus answers this by preaching His own enthronement in glory. Further, it is not impossible to see in verse 63 an objection and response. The early Gnostic movements, as is known from the letters of Ignatius of

6. Chapter V, "The New Testament," art. 19. See *The Documents of Vatican II,* Walter M. Abbot, general editor. New York, 1966, p. 124.

Antioch and other sources, refused to receive the Eucharist because they could not accept the incarnation. For them, the Son of God only took on the appearance of flesh, but was in fact completely spiritual. John addresses the words of Jesus to these "disciples": "The spirit gives life, the flesh is of no avail" [you say; but I say:] "the words that I have spoken to you" [". . . my flesh is food indeed and my blood is drink indeed"] "these are 'spirit and life.' " Thus, the rejection of the clear words of Jesus, giving His true body and blood, far from finding "the spirit which gives life," are a rejection of both "spirit" and "life." John indicates the situation in the Church when he states, "After this many of His disciples went back to where they formerly were and no longer walked about with Him" (6:66). John's somewhat cryptic way of saying that some of the disciples left Jesus is understandable in the context of the Gnostic claims to have found the new secret way to salvation. Their "new way" is actually a way back to where they used to be, lacking in salvation.

Thus, it is possible to see in this discourse the use of Jesus' actual deeds and words but a use which is tailored to the needs of the Church. The stimulus for this section of the gospel, which is an explanation of the miracle of the multiplication of loaves for the five thousand, would seem to be the Gnostic objections to the Eucharist. The gospel is affirming the real presence of Christ in the Eucharist itself, as it is celebrated daily in the Church. The whole setting of the multiplication of the loaves is set into the context of the Passover: "Now the Passover, the feast of the Jews, was at hand" (6:4). Jesus contrasts His action with the action of God in the Old Testament. In the old days, God gave the Jews bread from heaven, but they all died. Now God gives a new bread, the flesh of Jesus which is food indeed (6:31, 51).

The accounts of the synoptic gospels, in their sober narration of the events of the Last Supper, could appear to be "historical" in the sense that their purpose is simply the narration of what happened. But close study of the texts, as well as of St. Paul's presentation of the tradition which was given to him, has brought scripture scholars generally to the conclusion that the words of Jesus as narrated in these accounts have a *liturgical* origin.[7] Granted that this liturgical tradition is rooted in what actually took place in the Last Supper, the liturgical origins of the words of institution bring out an important dimension in what the gospels are saying. They are presenting the tradition concerning the Last Supper which had been preserved in the Church, it is true. But the vehicle which had preserved that tradition and the source of the evangelists' narration is the daily celebration of the Eucharist in the Christian communities. Benoit points out that Paul's account presents the liturgical tradition of Antioch, while Mark's seems to reflect the usage of the community of Jerusalem.[8] The accounts are both extremely jejune both in detail and in explanation of the meaning of the action of Jesus. But to the Christian communities, the meaning was clear enough from the setting into which the evangelists put their accounts. And it is from the setting of these accounts that they came to understand both what Jesus did at the Last Supper and what the Church does daily in her celebration of the Eucharist.

The synoptic gospels set the Last Supper in a context which has two directions of meaning. From what precedes the account of institution, it can be seen that the meaning of the Eucharist is to be found in the context of the meaning of Passover. From what follows, the meaning of the Eucharist is seen to be set in the context of the passion and death of Jesus. All these dimensions serve to clarify the meaning of one another. The Passion and Passover illuminate the meaning of the Last Supper (and thus of the Eucharist in the life of the Church), and the Last Supper explains the final direction of meaning incarnate in Passover and in the Passion narrative. In the Last Supper, Jesus said, "This is my body . . . This is my blood." But what is the meaning of this body and blood? From the twofold direction of meaning, it can be seen that this body and blood are sacrificial realities. The body of Christ takes on the meaning of the Unleavened Bread: communion in the paschal sacrifice, a sacrifice whose meaning and power are transformed in the sacrifice of the cross. The body

7. Jeremias, *op. cit.,* pp. 106 ff.; Benoit, *art. cit.,* pp. 72–73.
8. *Art. cit.,* p. 72.

of Christ is the body of Jesus who was crucified and who has risen. The blood of Christ, the "covenant blood," takes on the meaning of the blood of the paschal sacrifice, poured out at the foot of the altar. It is a sacrifice for the propitiation of sins, a sacrifice of covenant between God and man, a celebration of deliverance, an act in which God constitutes and gathers together a people. At the same time, the action of Jesus in the Last Supper gives the meaning and power of the Passion, an event which otherwise is simply a terrible physical fact for the beholder. The body of Jesus is a body which is not slain, but "given for you"; His blood is not simply poured out, but is poured out "on behalf of the many," "for the forgiveness of sins." And the command "Take and eat . . . Take and drink" is Christ's command to communicate in the meaning and power of His suffering, death and resurrection. Thus, the eating and drinking which is done in the Eucharist is sacramental communion in the sacrificial reality of Christ.

Thus the presence of Christ, the real presence, the true presence of Christ is absolutely central to the biblical faith in the meaning and power of the Eucharist. St. Paul brings this out in an addition to the accounts of institution which is absent in the others. He cites the words of Jesus, "Do this for my remembrance"([Lk 22:19]; 1 Cor 11:24) and, "Do this, as often as you drink, for my remembrance" (1 Cor 11:25). The Eucharist is the community's celebration of the power of Christ's redemptive act on the cross: "As often as you eat this bread and drink this cup, you are proclaiming the death of the Lord, until He comes" (v. 26). Just as Jesus proclaimed the sacrificial meaning and power which was before the members of the Last Supper in His body and blood, the Church proclaims this same sacrificial reality, present among them in "this bread" and "this cup." Further, Jeremias brings out a biblical dimension in these words of Jesus which gives them an even broader significance.[9] He points out that these words are a prayer that this might be done in the Church so that *God* would be mindful of Him. And

9. *Op. cit.*, pp. 237–255.

this understanding brings out the eschatological significance of the Eucharist, a meaning which corresponds to the treatment of the Letter to the Hebrews which stresses the fact that Christ has entered once and for all into heaven itself, now to appear on our behalf (9:24). Christ is God's gift of worship to man, a worship which is a participation-in-communion in the effective cultic reality of the Risen and Glorified Lord, seated at the right hand of majesty (8:1–2). Thus, not only is man celebrating the redemptive action of Jesus, but in this celebration, the sacrificial reality of Jesus is celebrated as He is before the Father, —a constant motive for God's remembrance of His promises, a constant prayer for the fulfillment of those promises. And the fulfillment of those promises will be human history "when He comes" (1 Cor 11:26).

Thus, the accounts of the institution of the Eucharist in the presentation of the events of the Last Supper are clearly stating the real presence of Christ. They are narratives which present the historical reality of the Last Supper, but their primary intention is not the simple historical narration of the event. Their primary interest is rather the presentation of that event as the foundation for the apostolic Church's understanding of what takes place in the Church's own Eucharistic celebration. They are, when understood in this broader historical context, a striking statement of the real presence of Christ in the Eucharist, not simply of His real presence at the Last Supper. They are, like so many aspects of the gospel narratives, not simply the narrative of the sayings and deeds of Jesus. They are this, to be sure. But the historical life of Jesus is presented as the basis for the meaning and power which is incarnate in the day-to-day life of the Church of the apostolic age. These narratives are ultimately speaking about the Eucharist here and now, not simply there and then. Like the events of the Old Testament, these events were "written down for our instruction" (1 Cor 10:11), preaching the meaning and power of the Eucharist to those who believe today. And in this preaching, so suggestively set in the light of the meaning of Passover, they preach to us the unity of our Eucharistic table with the "altar" which God has set up in Christ, establishing Him as the new "place of propitiation" in the blood which He shed and which we receive in faith (Rom 3:25).

A final consideration remains. It is the question of the character of the real presence of Christ in the Eucharist. In the theological elaboration of the real presence, the corollary to the statement of the real presence has often been the question of *what* is present in the Eucharist. The Council of Trent, following the lead of theology since the 12th century, stated that by the force of the words of consecration, the body and blood of Christ are present, but because of the immortality of the Risen Christ and because of the inseparable unity of the divine and human in Jesus, His soul and divinity are present. And thus the whole Christ is present under the appearances of bread and wine. Further, theologians and preachers have presented an explanation of the Eucharist in the light of this question which centers around the presence of Christ's action. The theology of the "mystery-presence" of Odo Casel is perhaps the best known of these explanations. Central to this theology is the conviction that the liturgical celebration of Christ's life somehow evokes the historical events of His life so that these events, these actions are now "present in mystery" at least to the extent that their religious power is present. Schillebeeckx rightly notes a subtle form of Docetism in this position pointing out that the true humanity of Jesus demands a genuine historicity in His life, that it be a life lived in the genuinely irreversible character of human history.[10] If these events and actions are genuinely historical, they took place once and cannot take place again. The same tendency is apparent in the preaching which is heard especially during the liturgy of Holy Week to the effect that the event of the Last Supper, the crucifixion, the resurrection are renewed in their celebration. The same question, "What is present?", is the source of a number of problems in scholastic theology concerning the "accidents" of Christ's glorified humanity. The question of the

10. E. Schillebeeckx, *Christ the Sacrament of the Encounter with God*, New York and London, 1963, pp. 54–59.

presence of the "quantity" of Christ's body exercised the ingenuity of many a theologian of the middle ages and beyond.

In all of these problems, the basic difficulty does not seem to be the answers, which are logical enough according to the principles of the various schools of theology, as much as the question itself. So often the history of theology has been the record of contrary answers to a question which it were better was never asked. Granted the question, the answers will follow the convictions of the school to which any given theologian belongs. Thus, when it is asked, "What is present in the Eucharist?", the answers, body and blood, soul and divinity, historical event, extension, a unique type of location, —these are logical. But it would seem far more in keeping with the principles of theological intelligibility to ask the question differently, viz., "*Who* is present?" For it is in the existential unity of the Incarnate Word that the real answer to the problem of the character of Christ's presence is best answered.

The question "Who is present in the Eucharist?" centers the theology of the Eucharist on the personal reality of Christ. And, in the light of Vatican I's principles of theological intelligibility, viz., that the most fruitful knowledge of the mysteries of faith comes from human analogies and the mutual connection between the mysteries of the Trinity, incarnation, Church and grace, this question places the theology of the Eucharist in a christological context, with the trinitarian and ecclesiological implications of this context. Further, this question also places the Eucharist in a more humanly intelligible framework, for acts and events can only be "present" in a given context to the extent that the person or persons who perform these acts and comprise these acts and events are present. For actions and events do not float free in history; they are the actions of persons and they are the events in which persons are essential to historical character. Trite as this might seem, it contains the answer to the meaning of the Eucharist as a whole, the preaching of the word, the change which takes place in the consecration, the meaning of communion and the sacrificial cast of these many moments within the one sacramental action of the Eucharist.

The personal reality of Christ is that of the Son of God incarnate in a real human history. But this implies two dimensions in the personal actions of Christ, dimensions which are implied in the expression "theandric actions." The life of Christ is both divine and human. Personally actualized by the reality of the Son of God, Christ's action is nevertheless authentically historical in the human sense. This means that, although the root of these actions is the timeless reality of the Son of God, they take place in the historical reality of the human situation. And this, in turn, means that although from one point of view the Son is all that He is or will ever be, His human life is authentically human, endowed with the genuine historicity of the human situation. And this means that Jesus is not simply a static human fact, but that His human vocation consists in becoming the man He is. This is expressed well in the hymn of the Letter to the Philippians when it is said that Jesus "*became* obedient" (2:8). The fact that Jesus is "the Lord" is not simply due to His being Son of God, possessing "equality with God," but is the fruit of the historical course of His life. What He is now, or better, who He is now, is also the fruit of the pattern of obedience which manifested His Sonship in human terms for man's salvation. It is because He was obedient "even to death" that Jesus is the Lord, to the glory of God of God the Father. But what does all this mean?

It means two things. First, in terms of the human life and vocation of Jesus, it means that His resurrection is the fruit of a whole life in which He manifested His Sonship in the constant obedience which He showed to the initiative of His Father. In other words, the human history of Jesus has made Him who He is now. Thus, if He is the Risen One, it is because He is the Crucified, laying down His life in the profession of His own Sonship. This dimension of the life of Jesus forms almost an antiphonal refrain in the gospel of John, the constant emphasis on the fact that the sayings and deeds of Jesus are the fruit of the initiative of the Father. It occurs in almost every chapter of John. This is who He is personally, and this is His confession to the end. John ends his gospel with the final and greatest beatitude,

"Blessed is the man who has not seen but has believed" (20:29). It is not a human life which is important, but the fact that this is the personal human manifestation of the Son of God for the salvation of man. It is the divine content in the life of Jesus which is the ultimate level of its meaning. It appeals not simply to historical analysis but to faith in which the Son of God is seen incarnate.

But at the same time, the human pattern of Jesus' life is important. And this is because Jesus did not simply appear in history as the Risen One, but became the Risen One through the pattern of His life and death. And thus, all that He is now, the Lord, is the fruit of the historical pattern of fidelity and obedience to His central mission, that of being the Son of God in a human way. Jesus, in other words, is not simply who He is, but He is who He has become, the Son of God who has lived out His human vocation to the full and thus become the "Son of God established in power" through His resurrection *from the dead* (Rom 1:4). Thus, the whole life of Jesus is important, because it is in His faithful obedience to His Father, even unto death, that He has become the Risen One, the Lord, the Christ, anointed with the Spirit.

On the other hand, this consideration of the genuine historicity of the life of Jesus and of the fact that He merited His resurrection must always be balanced by the fact that He is the Son of God. This gives a unique character to His personal human history. It means, after all, that the personal reality incarnate in this human life is not bound by the categories of human history for His own personal constitution. The human history of Jesus incarnates a person who is not subject to history as a person. And this means that the historical pattern of the genuinely historical life and death of Jesus contains a dimension of reality, meaning and power which is above and beyond history, a reality which can be called "trans-historical."[11] The actions of Jesus are actions which He performs in time, but the personal subject of these actions is the timeless actuality of the Son of God. And thus,

11. *Op. cit.,* p. 56.

though these actions are genuinely historical, they are also of a timeless, perennial character. What Jesus did in His human history is actual in His personal reality now. What Jesus did in the Last Supper, what He did on Calvary, what He did in the resurrection—all of this is actually real in His personal reality at this moment.

This is important for the understanding of the implications of the question "Who is present in the Eucharist?" in contrast with the question "What is present in the Eucharist?" For it is the personal reality of Christ which is present in the Eucharist, incarnate personal reality, to be sure, but personal reality nonetheless. And this means that, in the personal reality of Christ, there is present in the Eucharist the actuality of what took place in the Last Supper, Calvary and the resurrection to the extent that all of this is the timeless personal action of the Son of God in a human history. Thus, in one sense He is who He always was, Son of God, but at the same time, He is who He has become in a genuine human history, the Son of God incarnate in a truly historical human life all of which is perennially actual in His timeless personal existence.

### *The One Gift*

The personal presence of Christ, with all the salvific meaning and power which this implies, is the key to the understanding of both the unity and diversity of gifts in the Eucharist. For the personal reality of Christ is a unity in diversity. This is clear in the teaching of the Council of Chalcedon which insists on the fact that the human and divine are to be seen in Christ "unconfused, . . . undivided and inseparable, . . . preserving the particularity of each nature [human and divine] concurring in the one person and subsistence." The gift of communion in Christ in the gift which is one in His personal reality, but multivalent in the reality of the distinction in Christ of the divine and the human. Communion in Christ is the gift of His divine life truly incarnate in a human history.

Communion in Christ means that the Eucharist is the gift of

communion in the very life of Christ, for the man who receives Christ abides in Him and he in Christ. "As the living Father sent me and I live because of the Father, he who eats me will live because of me" (Jn 6:56–57). This is a gift of God's life, the life of Father, Son and Spirit. The theology of the Eucharist has centered around the personal reality of Christ, but it must be remembered that the distinction of persons in the Trinity does not mean that the persons of the Trinity are separable from one another. Quite to the contrary, the persons of the Trinity are inseparable from one another. The man who sees Christ thus sees the Father, and the man who receives Christ, receives the Father—and the Spirit. This consideration sets the mystery of the Eucharist against the mystery of the Trinity in the light of the definition of the XIth Council of Toledo. Enlarging on the definition of the Council of Nicea, the council insisted that, although the distinction of persons in the Trinity is true, this does not mean that the persons are separable. Rather, it means that the three persons are not to be considered separable since neither one exists before, after or without the others in the inexpressible unity of the divine nature. The gift of Christ is a gift from the Father and it a gift of the Spirit given in and through Christ.

But this gift of the life of Father, Son and Spirit is accomplished in the *human* reality of Christ, in the *incarnate* person of the Son. And this means that the personal reality of Christ is the timeless core of the actions of the Last Supper, Calvary and the resurrection. If the question is asked, then, what it is that makes the Eucharist a sacrifice, the answer is found in the fact that the Eucharist is communion in the personal reality of Christ. The Letter to the Hebrews stresses the perennial sacrificial reality of Christ, emphasizing the human historical action in which this sacrifice was realized and, at the same time, emphasizing the perennial actuality of that sacrifice. On the one hand, Christ had to *learn* obedience and through this become the source of salvation to all who obey Him (5:7–10), but at the same time, once He offered His life, He had put away sin once and for all, sanctified all men once and for all, perfecting for all time those who are to be sanctified by a single offering (9:26; 10:10–15). The value of this single offering is not in the fact that it is better because it is somehow greater than any other human offering. Its value is in the fact that this is an offering made by the Son of God, in union with the Father and the Spirit. This is an offering which is given to man by God in Christ. It is an offering which is infallibly acceptable to God. It is an offering which unfailingly achieves the authenticity of worship which no human act can achieve, because it is a divine act of worship incarnate in the events of the life and death of Christ. Thus, the Eucharistic presence of Christ is of and in itself a sacrificial presence. Sacrifice and sacrament are not two gifts in the Eucharist. They are one—one in the personal reality of Christ.

Because of the historical stress which has been placed on the diverse dimensions of sacrament and sacrifice in the Eucharist, the Eucharist has come to be presented as two realities, the sacramental presence of Christ and the sacrificial action achieved in the consecration. The historical statements of the Church have been and remain significant. But the theological appreciation of the Eucharist demands that the Eucharist be set against its background in the theology of the Trinity and the incarnation. And from this point of view, the unifying principle between the Eucharist, Trinity, incarnation and Church can be found in the mediating function of Christ. Mediation is the central content of the incarnation, and in different contexts it has different characteristics. Thus, for example, in the context of the sinful human situation, the incarnation is God's action of redemption of man in Christ. St. Paul emphasizes this in his statement that God was in Christ reconciling the world to Himself (2 Cor 5:18–19). In the context of God's righteousness, His absolute fidelity to His promises, Christ's function of mediation is expressed in terms of satisfaction. St. Paul develops this aspect of Christ's mediation in his contrast between the effect of Adam's sin and Christ's life and death, stating that the judgment of death reigned because of one man's sin, but in Christ God has given men the gift of reigning in life (Rom 5:16–17). Finally, in the context of man's call to worship God in Spirit and Truth, God's gift to man in Christ is the gift of an authentic worship, a perfect and abiding sacrifice in which man can express that life of worship which is only authentic in God's gift (Hebr cc. 5, 7–10). Thus, in Christ's action, God gives man a cultic mediator, but this is only one aspect of the universal mediating function of Christ. His sacrifice is perfect; it needs no repetition because He continues to be that sacrifice forever: He "always lives to make intercession" (Hebr 7:25).

All of these manifold aspects of the personal reality of Christ, however, are facets of the one central function of Christ, "For there is one God, and there is one mediator between God and men, the man Christ Jesus, who gave Himself as a ransom for all . . ." (1 Tim 2:5). Although no motive can be assigned *a priori* for this mediating function, some intelligibility of it is possible in the light of the personal relations which constitute the persons of the Trinity. In this context, the personal reality of the Son is that of being derived from the Father. The Son exists in that He is proceeding from, generated by the Father. And, though the Father is not derived from the Son, He is constituted as a person by His relation to the Son. It is the personal reality and function of the Son to be the image, the word, the perfect self-expression of the Father. This relationship escapes analysis, because of the fact that while the Father generates the Son as Father, we cannot conceive of the action of generation except by the person of the Father, who, in turn, is only constituted as a person by His relationship to the Son. But, in spite of this, the revealed personality of the Son is to be the image and word of the Father. The personal reality of the Spirit is constituted by a relation to Father and Son alike. For the Spirit subsists as the person who is the love of Father and Son, binding Father and Son in the ineffable unity of the divine nature. The personal reality and function of the Spirit is to be the bond between persons.

These personal realities and functions are essential to the understanding of the incarnation. As a person, the Son assumes a relation to an individual human nature, He becomes man, the man Jesus. But the meaning and value of His life extends far beyond the individuality of His own human existence. This is not so much because, as some theologians would maintain, somehow all men are "included" in the human individuality of Jesus. Rather, it is because in the inseparable unity of the divine nature, the Son remains united to the Spirit even in the incarnation. Jesus comes into the world anointed with the Spirit.

The gospels state this theme variously. Matthew and Luke associate this union of Christ and the Spirit with the episode of the Baptism. In this theophany, God manifests His Son to the world and anoints Him with the Spirit. In Mark's gospel, Jesus appears on the scene with the Spirit and that Spirit begins His struggle against the spirit of evil from the very start of the gospel. John begins his gospel in the same vein, proclaiming Jesus as the "Lamb of God, who takes away the sin of the world" (1:29), placing the appearance of Jesus in the context of the expectation of the outpouring of the Spirit of righteousness in the last days, which is the sign of the final judgment: the forgiveness of sins. Paul develops this theme more explicitly in a theology in which the full reality of Christ's Sonship appears in the resurrection, in which Christ is "established as Son of God in power according to the Spirit of holiness through His resurrection from the dead" (Rom 1:4), so that as the first Adam became a living being, the last Adam became a life-giving spirit (1 Cor 15:45).

One can see in this anointing of Jesus with the Spirit any number of mediating missions. Jesus Himself explains it in terms of a prophetic anointing in which He is given the mission associated in Isaiah with the outpouring of the Spirit: the mission of mediating God's word to man, of "preaching the good news to the poor" (Lk 4:18; Is. 61:1–2). But if the union of the Spirit with Jesus is looked at from the point of view of the personal reality and function of the Spirit, the central import of this anointing can be seen to be that of uniting the incarnate person of Christ with other persons through the mediation of His humanity. The anointing of Jesus with the Spirit, in other words, makes the man Jesus the ontological mediator between God and man. This means that God does not simply act "as if" all men are in Christ, "as if" His death is a death which is literally in the name of and in the place of all men. In the anointing of Jesus with the Spirit, His life and death and resurrection are really and objectively for all men. St. Paul stresses this with striking clarity in the hymn which opens the Letter to the Ephesians blessing God for giving men every blessing in Christ before the foundation of the world, for choosing men in Christ. For this reason men have redemption, the forgiveness of sins *in* Christ. Indeed, God's whole plan is simply to unite everything in Christ, the head and the source of all creation (Eph 1:3–10). The hymn in the Letter to the Colossians simply states that everything is created through Christ and toward Christ. The whole constitution of the supernatural order takes place concretely in the creation of men in direction toward the "fullness" of Christ (Col 1:15–20). The gift of God's own life which is the central reality of "grace" is given to man in Christ Jesus. This is the heart of His mediating function. He is, in a real though mystical way, the whole of mankind, and for this reason all men are redeemed in Him.

Jesus Himself expresses this in a cultic context when He associates Himself with the sacrificial death of the "Servant of Yahweh" by saying that the purpose of His coming is to "give His life as a ransom for the 'many' " (Mk 10:45; Is 53:10 ff.). There is a temptation, especially in the theology of the Eucharist, to disassociate this cultic reality from the life of Jesus and attach it only to His death. This leads to the conviction that it is the sacrifice of Calvary which is present in the Eucharist. But such a view overlooks a fundamental fact, viz., that true sacrifice is only such in the context of an authentic worship. And authentic worship finds its authenticity not in cultic gesture and formula, but in the fact that these acts of worship are the authentic expression of a life of worship which is brought to ceremonial cult and expressed therein. Without this existential content in the life of the worshipper, worship becomes mere ceremony devoid of real content. Thus, the death of Christ can only be seen to be sacrificial in the context of the authentic worship which is at the core of His whole life. This is the ultimate and definitive affirmation of His relationship to God in the act of laying down His life. And it is only true to the extent that the human life of Jesus is a constant and unvarying action of authentic worship, the unceasing affirmation of who He is before God. John's gospel stresses this reality in Jesus' life with particular clarity. The theme of the fidelity of Jesus to the initiative of the Father is an antiphonal refrain echoed in almost every chapter and climaxed in Jesus' affirmation in the last discourse that He has "sanctified" Himself so that His disciples might also be sanctified in truth (17:19). This expression is a translation of a Hebrew expression whose meaning seems to have been lost, but which refers to the ritual in which a man is installed as a priest. In Jesus' discourse, this "sanctifying" is the expression of something which has been in the life of Jesus from the beginning, viz., His fidelity to the work which the Father has given Him to do (Jn 17:4). This Jesus has accomplished and this accomplishment is the heart and soul of Jesus' worship of the Father, a worship in which Jesus has consecrated Himself, but not only Himself; He has consecrated Himself so that "they" (His disciples and those who will come to believe through them), too, might be "sanctified in truth." Thus, the sanctification of the disciples means basically that the disciples come to share in the fidelity of the whole life of Jesus which is affirmed so definitively in His death, for it is precisely on their behalf, in their name and in their place that Jesus sanctified Himself by His life of fidelity. They come to share, then, in the whole content of the personal history of Jesus.

All this serves to illustrate the fact that worship is not an isolated reality. It is woven into the whole fabric of life. It is the faithful living out of the vocation of being God's creature. Only to the extent that this actually is the content of a life can ceremonial worship have any real content. In this context, it can be seen that the death of Jesus can only be called "sacrifice" to the extent that His entire life is a life of authentic worship in His absolute fidelity to the central work given to Him by the Father: bringing the life of God to man by living as the Son of God in a human way on behalf of and in the name of the "many." The cultic dimension of the life of Jesus is seen in looking at the life of Jesus from this point of view. It is not something disparate or disassociated from the whole pattern of His life. His entire *life,* heavenly and earthly, is His *worship* of the Father.

This has an important implication for the theology of the Eucharist. And this is the fact that the Eucharist is not a number of gifts: the presence of Christ, sacrifice, communion. The Eucharist is one gift. It is God's gift of a worship which man cannot achieve of himself. It is a worship given to man in Christ Jesus, the one mediator between God and man in whom every gift of grace is contained on man's behalf. In the personal reality of Jesus man has redemption from sin, satisfaction for trespasses, a sacrifice forever pleasing and effective before God. For this is God's only-begotten Son in whom He is well-pleased. The personal presence of Christ in the Eucharist is in itself a sacrifice. The one gift of Christ is a gift of every blessing in the one mediator of God and man.

The Eucharist is not a gift of a death. It is a gift of a life, the unfailing life of the Risen Christ. It is that life which is the gift of worship, of sacrifice. It is the gift of Christ who is and always will be the sacrificial reality He has made Himself in His life, death and resurrection. And this consideration brings out the heart of the meaning of the Eucharist. This is an act of worship which is performed by Christ, but in which He associates the whole of His body with Himself in giving glory to the Father. But this gift of worship is not simply the gift of an isolated action. It is not simply the gift of an act of worship. It is rather the gift of a whole way of life which comes to expression in this one action. It is the continued gift of the life of the body of Christ, given anew in each celebration of the mystery of that body. In continuity with the Jewish celebration of Passover, the Christian Pasch is the gift of life and unity to a people whom God gathers together in Christ's body through the continual outpouring of the one Spirit who is one and the same in Christ and in the Christian.

The biblical faith in the Eucharist, then, is a faith in the real presence of Christ which is affirmed in terms of the events of the Last Supper, but this affirmation is directed primarily toward the meaning and value of the celebration of the Christian Pasch daily in the Church. This is a sacrificial presence because it is the presence of the Risen Christ in the Eucharistic community under the appearances of bread and wine. It is sacrificial in that Christ Himself, the one mediator between God and man, offers this worship to His Father and ours, associating the whole of His body, the Church, in this perfect act of worship. And the central reality in this act of worship is the body of Christ, His undying human reality in which the Son of God subsists, offering endless worship to the Father. But this worship is not simply aimed at one act of the Church associated with Christ. In the gift of Christ, this Eucharist is a gift of the very life of the Church itself. It is the gift of the Christ and His Spirit who are the life and mystery of the Church. It is a gift which binds the Church into a unity in Christ through His Spirit. Its power goes beyond the act of ceremonial worship to the day-to-day life of the Christian in the Church. It is the gift of the forgiveness of sins, the bond of unity, the pledge of a life which has no ending. As Christ has lived, died and risen for all of mankind, those who eat shall live because of Christ, forever.

The restriction of the theology of the Eucharist to the reality of Christ's presence and the reality of the sacrificial value in the Eucharist loses sight of the broader meaning of the Eucharist for the whole life of the Church. This is *the* act of the Church in which, associated with her heavenly Head, she celebrates the mystery of her unity in Him and receives this unity from the Father in the gift of Christ and His Spirit. The Church lives out of the Eucharist. It is above all in the Eucharist that God fills up the "fullness of Christ" as a pledge of that final fullness in which all things will be gathered together in Him.

This broader understanding of the meaning and power of the Eucharist is not absent in the gospel theologies of the Eucharist. John's theology of the Eucharist has been seen to associate the meaning and power of the Eucharist with the narrative of the multiplication of the loaves. In the discourse on the Bread of Life which serves as a commentary on this miracle, the Eucharist emerges as the ultimate test of the unity of the Church. In their rejection of the Eucharist many of the "disciples" are seen to walk away and abandon the faith which saves. Mark makes use of the feeding of the five thousand to begin a series of sacramental themes which are closed by the feeding of the four thousand (6:30—8:10). The first feeding takes place in Galilee and the second takes place in the Decapolis after a sojourn among the Gentiles in which there are the incidents of the curing of the daughter of the Syro-Phoenician woman (7:24-30), the healing of the dumb man by the "*Ephphatha*" (a hint at Baptism). The objections of the Pharisees in chapter 7 bring out the conflict between Jew and Gentile in the Church which is mentioned in the Acts of the Apostles (c. 15). Mark treats of this in his comment that all foods were declared clean by the words of Jesus (7:19). But in a more sacramental context, Mark presents the Eucharist as the bond of unity between Jew and Gentile by presenting the picture of the one Jesus feeding the multitudes among Jews and Gentiles alike. Matthew suggests this same theme in a gospel which is more oriented toward a theology of the missionary Church in his setting of these miracles between the great parables on the Church (c. 13) and the confession of Peter at Caesarea Philippi (16:13–32). The function of the incidents in Matthew does not possess the same emphasis on unity, but it is strongly related to the constitution of the Church.

The biblical faith in the meaning of the Eucharist, then, contains a strong statement of the real presence of Christ in the Eucharist as it is celebrated in the Church. It places this presence in a clear sacrificial context in the Last Supper. But it also speaks of the meaning of this presence of Christ. It is a presence which unites the Church in Him, the constant gift of the very life of the Church in Christ, her Head.

CHAPTER THREE

# THE SACRAMENT OF THE EUCHARIST

THIS study has attempted thus far to present the historical changes of emphasis which have taken place in the theological treatment of the Eucharist and the liturgical experience of the Eucharist. It has then passed to an attempt at the statement of the biblical faith in the Eucharist in order to situate the questions of the real presence and the sacrificial value of the Eucharist in the broader theology of the Eucharist which is found in the New Testament. With this foundation, it passes to a more specifically theological treatment of the Eucharist as a sacrament. Only after this has been analyzed can there be any satisfactory presentation of the current debate on the Eucharist and the questions of the contemporary appreciations of the real presence and of "transsubstantiation" and "transsignification."

## *A Sacrament is a Sign-Act*

The Council of Trent resumed centuries of theology in its statement on the sacramental character of the Eucharist: "It is common to the Eucharist and to the rest of the sacraments 'to be the symbol of a sacred thing and the visible form of invisible grace' " (DS 1639). The Augustinian tradition in sacramental theology, emphasizing the sign-dimension in the sacrament, was eventually fused with the scholastic efforts at definition in Peter Lombard's *Book of Sentences,* with the distinction between the sacraments of the New Law and those of the Old Law being placed in the *efficacy* of the Christian sacrament. This definition gave a bipolar character to the study of the sacrament. The sacrament was treated as a sign and as a cause, and the integration of these two dimensions in the theology of the sacraments became the challenge to theology for the next seven hundred years. The Reformation, with its insistence on the sacraments as signs of the faith of the believer, served to demand all the more emphasis on the sacrament as a cause of grace. From that time on, the emphasis in the speculative theology of the sacraments has been on the elaboration of a number of different theories of sacramental causality. Only a few theologians undertook the task of attempting to integrate the dimensions of sign and cause in their speculation. John of St. Thomas seems to have been one of the more successful in this enterprise. The value of his and other treatments, however, is always seen in the light of the intellectual convictions of different schools of thought. Some would consider it successful and valid; others would reject it. In general, however, it can be said that opinion generally divides into two large groups. The first, claiming to represent the authentic tradition of St. Thomas, stresses the efficient causality of the sacrament as the instrument in the causing of grace. The other, reflecting more the nominalist theological tradition, tends to develop a "moral bond" of some kind between the sacramental action and the "production of grace."

To the mind which is somewhat detached from the convictions of particular schools, however, there emerges a certain basic identity in these large divisions of opinion. This identity lies in the fact that both accept a common state of the question. Thus, the sacrament is considered as a sign, and a sign is a thing which presents itself to the senses but which conveys to the mind the knowledge of something else—in this case, grace. The application of this definition to the sacraments, then, views the sacrament as a *thing* which has a logical or gnoseological relation to another *thing,* grace. Various systems of thought will devise various kinds of bonds between this one thing (the sign) and the other thing (grace). But what is common to both systems is the fact that the sacrament is seen as a *thing* and grace is seen as another *thing*. The theological enterprise becomes the task of somehow joining these two things together. Not that this is a conscious and deep conviction of either position. If one were to ask, "Do you really believe that grace is a thing?", some would answer, "Obviously not," while others, depending on how closely they were tied with the purity of the nominalist tradition, would agree that grace is indeed a thing which somehow must be linked to the sacrament. But the treatment emerges much the same. This treatment has been characterized by theologians given to the use of contemporary thought-forms as "mechanistic" in that it views the sacrament as a mechanism (granted, some kind of divine mechanism) for the production of grace, and as "dualistic" in that it sees the sacrament and the reality of grace as two disparate things.

It should be apparent that the solution to this problem does not simply lie in the formulation of a new philosophy of the sign. And this is not what has taken place in the theology of the Eucharist. Basic to the solution of the problem is the elaboration of a new theology of grace itself which, rather than viewing grace as a thing which is the "adornment of the soul," sees grace against the background biblical formulation of grace as the *action* which God has historically taken to share His own life with man. This means that the theology of grace is not simply stated in an individual theological treatise. It means that grace must be seen as the whole history of God's action accomplished in Christ and continued in the Church and her sacramental action in a visible form through the Spirit which binds the Church to Christ. As Christ is the very visibility of God's gracious action in history, the Church continues, in her sacramental action above all, to be that same gracious action realized in the present for man. Against this background, the reality of grace is seen to be the initiative of love which God takes on man's behalf, sharing His life with man ultimately in Christ and in the earthly body which is joined to Christ by the personal action of the one Spirit in Christ and the Christian. The basic reality of grace is God's gracious initiative. But this has an effect in man, giving him the capacity to live on a level which transcends human possibilities. Man can come to live with God in Christ through the Spirit. Man comes to see a meaning in his life which comes from his response to God's initiative in faith. Man's expectations from his own life take on the dimension of the divine in hope. Man's life becomes a life of personal relationship to God which is in a relationship between Creator and creature otherwise impossible: the relationship of love. All this is the situation of grace. It is unfortunate that the English language does not have the capacity to express this reality as other languages do. German and Dutch, for example, have an active verb which expresses this as the action in which God "graces" man (German: *begnadigen;* Dutch: *begenadigen*). The use of this kind of language readily dissipates the "objectifying" of grace which treats the reality of grace as a static entity, the *ornatus animae,* and brings to the consideration of grace the corrective of the dynamics of personal relationships.[1]

The stimulus for this appreciation of the reality of grace has been manifold, but perhaps the greatest stimulus for it has been the renewed appreciation of the scripture which has come from the rapid developments in scriptural studies and in biblical theology. Promising as this development has been, however, it could well have been stillborn were it not for the fact that the emergence of new thought-forms has accompanied it with remarkable coincidence.

The existentialist style of thought emerged in the 19th century as a reaction to the excessive rationalism of the German idealist movement. The post-Kantian view of man and his situation conceived of man as a being radically incapable of relating in any genuine way to anything beyond his own interior states. Neither the Kantian mechanics, the Hegelian dialectic nor the Cartesian inner awareness actually bridged the gap created by rationalism between man and his world. The existentialist revolt rejected this view of man by conceiving of man and the human situation as interrelated of themselves. For existentialism, the world is not a

1. Examples of this can be seen in P. Fransen's *Divine Grace and Man,* New York, 1965, and Schillebeeckx's *Christ the Sacrament of the Encounter with God,* pp. 3–6 (see Ch. 2, note 10, on p. 56).

reality in which there is an irreconcilable divorce between the conscious and the quantified. Rather, the real situation is one in which man's whole reality is directed toward his world for its reality and its growth. Man does not have to "go outside" to reach his world; man's world enters so deeply into man that it really is "his world." And human existence is a question of man's growing into his own human reality precisely by relating meaningfully to the world of persons and things in which he lives. Authentic human existence is essentially human growth: "being a man is becoming a man." And becoming a man is not simply the passive absorption of influences from "the outside," but consists in man's self-expression to the world of persons and things which surrounds and penetrates his own personal reality. Being a man is becoming a man, but becoming a man is essentially a process of self-expression to the world, a process in which man gives himself to his world and grows in the very giving.

From the outset, then, the existentialist view of man places man in a "symbolic" situation. In order to be a person, man must express himself, his own personal reality to his world. This means that man's interior reality must be incarnated in bodily signs, speech and gesture. And through the bodily dimension of his existence, man assumes the material world into the function and growth of his very personal reality. And in this assumption, the material world is itself transformed into the personal reality which it comes to express. Thus, man's world is not only the term and goal of his growth. It is also the very means and terms of his growth as a person. The reason for this is that man's personal reality is not an abstract blank. Rather, it is an essential orientation toward a real world, and the functioning of the person, the "growth to the outside," takes place in terms of the world which is one of the poles of man's consciousness. Man is conscious of himself in terms of his world and the history of his life in his world. The very dynamics of personal reality and function, then, are to be seen in the symbolic functioning of the human person. A man only knows who he is to the extent that he knows what he has made himself to be in a concrete individual history lived out in a real world which has been really effected by his historical action and which has been the stimulus, content and goal of his history.

The process of human growth, then, which is the existential functioning of the human person, is, in its essence, a process of sign-acts, acts in which man expresses his own personal reality to his world and thus grows into his own personal reality. In this view of man, human bodiliness is itself the *sign* of personal reality. For it is through the bodily dimension of human existence that man gives himself to his world, and it is through this same dimension that man's world penetrates his personal reality.[2] Karl Rahner points out, however, that the symbolic function of the body is not to be viewed dualistically, even in the authentic tradition of Thomism. For if the soul is seen as the "substantial form" of the body, this means that the soul is the very actuality of the body, and the body, in turn, is the very self-expression of the soul, but which, at the same time is existentially one with the soul, an expression which takes place in that which is "other" than the soul, but which, at the same time is existentially one with the soul.[3] Thus, in the sign-acts in which man expresses his personal "interior" to the world, there is a fundamental unity in the sign (bodily action in which every part of man's body expresses his whole self) and what it "signifies" (viz., the interiority of man actualized in bodily action).

All of this is important for the understanding of what "meaning" is. It can be seen that meaning is not simply a value which the mind assigns to the elements of a situation. Meaning is rather the basic mutual relationship between man and the world in which he exists. Meaning is the basic value which man's world has for him and which he has for it. Man cannot create this value, because it is an aspect of the very givenness of man's being in his world. It is true that man can create the value of his "signals," but he cannot create the values which face him in his

2. M. Merleau-Ponty, *The Phenomenology of Perception,* New York and London, 1962, pp. 67–174. See also Mary Rose Barral, *Merleau-Ponty: The Role of the Body-Subject in Interpersonal Relations,* Pittsburgh, 1965; and Karl Rahner, S.J., "Zur Theologie des Symbols," in *Schriften zur Theologie,* Vol. IV, Einsiedeln, 1960, pp. 275 ff.

3. *Art. cit.,* pp. 304 ff., especially pp. 306–308.

world. They are simply there. A man can say, "When I snap my fingers, sit down," but he cannot say, "Although I mean to love my son, I will rear him in hate and he will be a loving person." The human mind cannot assign the value of nourishment to arsenic and cyanide or attach the value of love to a bomb sent through the mail. The values of man and his world are too real, too objective, too given, and if they are ignored, they will inexorably take their toll. Insanity was once considered diabolical possession. Today it is recognized as the terrible attrition which one life can and must take on another.

On the other hand, it must be said that the world has no meaning apart from the human mind. For, granted all the God-given values which exist in the world, they only make up a capacity for meaning which is actual only when the human person functions in the world. It is man's function to realize the meaning of the world in its direction toward himself and God. And it is only in man's functioning as a person, living and growing in self-expression and self-giving to his world, that the objective potentiality of man's world to have actual meaning becomes existentially operative.

This view of man, then, sees man's life in its existential reality and functioning as a continuous "symbolization" of his own personal reality to his world. And it is important to note that what is "symbolized" to the world is man's own personal reality as this is active and informed by the reality of the world about him. Man's self-expression expresses man's self. But as tautological as this may sound, it is important to remember that the very selfhood of man is dependent on the world in which he really lives. This is the content of his personal being and it all comes to expression in the essential life-act of self-expression and self-giving. Thus, symbolic action is not simply the act of seeing one thing and thinking about something else. Symbolic action is rather the act of giving and receiving a personal reality which is incarnate in a bodily sign which, while it is not the totality of personal reality, is nonetheless the very appearance of personal reality to the world of persons and things which surrounds a man. Meaning is not assigned to these actions "from the outside."

Meaning is rather incarnate in these actions themselves. The personal reality which is the central meaning of man's symbolic action is the whole reason for the very actuality of these actions, and it is the goal of these actions. Man expresses himself to his world in order to be himself and to become himself.

Further, it can be seen that symbolic action is not a simple thing. It is, in fact, quite complex. The organ of self-expression is man's own bodiliness. But through this organ, man takes up any number of other material objects into the process of self-expression. People send flowers, give rings, serve meals, shoot guns, write letters, draw designs, do a thousand things in which the material world becomes the bearer of part or all of man's personal reality. What it is important to note, however, is that in the multiplicity of objects which make up any given sign-act, there is an essential unity in the act in the meaning which is incarnate in all these elements. It is the central meaning which makes the act one. And in this unity there takes place what Schillebeeckx refers to as a certain "pregnant alienation" of the individual realities involved in personal self-expression.[4] Material objects are robbed of their physical individuality by the fact that they are taken up into man's sign-acts and laden with man's personal reality. A gun in a store window rests in its own physical reality, but in the hands of a killer it becomes the effective expression of his fear, hate or greed. Canvas and oil, drafting pens and paper, paper and ink are robbed of their physical reality in their assumption into the act of conveying insight, intelligence or emotion from one person to others. They remain themselves physically, it is true, and they can all be subjected to physical examination and be found to be paper, canvas, oil and so on. But their existential reality in the human sign-act is that of the symbolic instrument which literally and

4. *Christus, Sacrament van de Godsontmoeting,* Bilthoven, 1961 (3rd ed.), p. 79. The English translation omits this expression. A translation of the sentence on p. 76 of the Sheed and Ward edition of 1963 with this expression would read: "In its human reality, of course, the symbol-act of the Church is a reality which clearly is genuinely 'separate' from Christ, which at the same time is *sacramentally* identified (and in this case, therefore, in pregnant *alienation* [*vervreemding*]) with the active heavenly body of Christ."

effectively incarnates the human person. All these elements *are* the personal reality they express, effectively incarnating and expressing that reality to man's world. Once again, it can be said that a gun is a gun and remains a gun even in the hands of a madman. But in such a situation, one does not avert to the physical reality of the gun as such. Rather, one effectively feels the reality of the madness it conveys, and runs. To do otherwise is either an attempt to ignore the danger or the sheerest foolishness.

This anthropological approach to the reality of the sign-act also illustrates the power of the sign-act. There is some truth to the view which situates the sign-act on the level of knowledge, seeing in the sign-act a vehicle for the communication of ideas. But this view of the sign-act deprives it of its more total power, a power which can be seen in the existentialist view of the symbolic situation. The sign-act conveys more than knowledge. It conveys the reality of the human person to another person. In the sign-act the total personal reality of one person reaches out to another in a total personal posture of love, hate or any of the myriad of personal attitudes. And what is incarnate in the sign-act is not simply the idea of love or hate; it is rather love or hate itself with all the power of the one who loves or hates to evoke the total personal response of the one to whom the sign-act is directed. Knowledge is, of course, a moment of this act, but its meaning and power are far more all-embracing. For it bears the whole history which has made this person to be this very particular person at this moment and directs this totality toward another historical human being. Thus, for example, the kiss of an elderly couple has a meaning and power far different from that of the newly married. The kiss of the faithful husband evokes the love of his wife, while that of the unfaithful husband evokes her disgust. Signs are indeed effective far beyond the realm of ideas, and their power lies precisely in their signifying. For what is contained in the sign is the person.

### *Sacraments Cause Grace by "Signifying" Grace*

Against this background, then, it is possible to approach with some understanding the reality of the sacramental act, the act which is the "sign of grace." Though it has been customary to restrict the content of the word "sacrament" to the ritual life of the Church, theologians for some time have been broadening the content of this word to include the reality of the Church itself, the foreshadowing of the Church in the Old Testament and, above all, Christ Himself. Since the time of Matthias Scheeben, Christ has been named "*Ursakrament,*" the primal sacrament, the sign of grace in terms of whom there is any other sign of grace. And this usage has found its way into the documents of Vatican II. In the *Dogmatic Constitution on the Church,* the council speaks of the Church as the "sacrament . . . of union with God and of the unity of the whole human race" (art. 1) and in the *Constitution on the Sacred Liturgy* the whole Church is called "the wondrous sacrament" (art. 5). This way of speaking is, in fact, a return to the patristic way of speaking of the Church and of Christ, which, in turn, is a reflection of St. Paul's use of *mustérion,* which the first Latin versions of the bible translated as either *mysterium* or *sacramentum.* The content of this word in the scriptures and the patristic writings corresponds to what has just been seen in the presentation of the reality of grace and that of the sign-act. For "sacrament" means the entire historical reality of God's gracing of man.[5]

The reality of grace, as has been seen, is basically that of God's sharing His life with man. This means that man's life, a constant created gift of God, is meant to share in the personal life of the Trinity, that man is meant to be God's son in Christ through the mediation of the Spirit. And this means that God reveals Himself to man personally and calls man to a personal relationship. One could speculate about the different ways in which God could possibly have brought all this about. But the fact is that God has brought it about by entering into man's history. God's creative love, in other words, has taken a visible shape in man's history in the perfect self-expression which God has in Christ, the "image of the invisible God, the first-born of all creation" (Col 1:15). And

5. See Schillebeeckx, *De sacramentele Heilseconomie,* Anvers, 1952, pp. 21–235, "De Historiek van de Sacramentsbepaling," esp. Ch. 1, "Benadering van het wezen van het sacrament langs de semantiek van de christelijke benaming *mustérion* en 'sacramentum.' "

God has given to man the gift of His Spirit, one and the same person in Christ and in mankind, who binds men to Christ in the mysterious unity of the body of Christ. And all of this historical (and history-making) action of God can be seen to be the divine counterpart to what has been seen to be the sign-act. For within the earthly visibility of the life of Jesus, it is God who is acting. And thus, it can be seen that Jesus is *the* "sign of grace." He is the act in whom God expresses himself perfectly to man, with all the power which is involved in God's own self-expression. Jesus is *the* "visible form of invisible grace." He is *the* sacrament. He contains in Himself, in the words of the Council of Trent, "the grace He signifies," i.e., His personal reality as the perfect self-expression of the Father is the core of His human life so that in that life God is perfectly expressed to man in history.

However, as has been seen, the human life of Jesus has a content of meaning and value beyond the individuality of Jesus. Because of His possession of the Spirit in the unity of God, the life of Jesus is a life in which God has gathered together a people, gathered them together precisely in the gift of the one person of the Spirit who is in Christ and the Christian. Through the mediation of this one Spirit Christ and the Church are one, so that even though the life of the Church on earth is genuinely earthly and historical, its life and action are at the same time the acts of Christ. And thus, hidden at the core of the life of the earthly Church is the divine reality of the Risen Christ who acts in and through the Church to realize the salvation He has gained for man. And thus, as Christ is the "sign of grace," the "visible form of invisible grace," the Church has this same sacramental character of incarnating God's gift of His own life in an earthly visibility. In the bond of the Spirit, the Church is sacramentally identified with her Head, Christ. And for this reason, the Church is a "sacrament," God's self-expression in Christ continued in history through the bond of the Spirit.

This is the basis of the power of the sacramental action of the Church. At its roots this action of the Church is the action of Christ who is sacramentally present to the world in the Church. This is the meaning of the expression "*ex opere operato,*" an expression of the objective power of the sacraments which basically means that Christ is truly present in the action of the Church because of her sacramental identity with Him in being and action. Of course, this does not mean that everything that happens in the Church is the action of Christ. History demonstrates all too clearly that the Church does not share the sinlessness of Christ completely. What it does mean, however, is that the action in which the Church, in union with Christ in the Spirit, seeks the grace of redemption from the Father, is one in reality with Christ's continuous intercession, and therefore is the very presence of Christ among men. And from this point of view, it can be seen that the "sacramental action of the Church" involves more than her public ceremonial worship. Her preaching is Christ's word living among men. Her works of charity make Christ's charity present. Her prayer is the prayer of Christ, laden with the power of Christ's prayer.

But if this is true of the life which the Church leads in sacramental union with Christ in her preaching, works of charity and prayer, it is true par excellence of the cultic sacraments: cultic actions in which the Church expresses her oneness with Christ more than in any other aspect of her life. For these actions are the actions in which, as Rahner has put it, the Church fulfills her very essence in the self-expression of her own mysterious "interiority."[6] And this "interiority," the essence, the heart of the Church's reality is that of the presence—indeed the "real" presence—of Christ to the world. It is in the cultic sacraments of the Church that the gracious initiative of God "graces" man here and now. It does not sanctify man in any mechanistic sense of the word, but it is the gracious love of God expressed to man in the visibility of the act of the Church. This is a visible invitation to man to accept and appropriate God's initiative in his own life and bring the full reality of grace to its full functioning in a genuine interpersonal love between God and man.

All this serves to clarify what St. Thomas Aquinas meant when he described the power of the sacrament by saying "they

6. *The Church and the Sacraments,* New York and London, 1963, pp. 21–24.

cause by signifying."[7] In the light of what has been seen concerning "sign-act" and "grace," it can be seen that the reality of grace is brought about in the sacraments because they are the acts in which God makes His own salvific reality present and operative in the visibility of the act of the Church which is one with Christ in the Spirit. Because of this sacramental bond between Christ and the Church, the sacrament is Christ's act, the sign-act in which He conveys His own salvific reality to the believer as the objective invitation to personal response. In Christ's own sign-act the objective reality of grace is present to man. The sacrament is the very visible shape of God's saving power offered to man in Christ. Every sign may not be a cause and vice versa, but the authentic sign of grace is the "cause of grace," at least in its objective presence, and vice versa, because it is Christ who is the "sign" in question and the cause at the same time. As Schillebeeckx has stated, "The gift of grace entails its own visibility."[8]

## *The Sacrament of the Eucharist*

The Council of Trent sets the Eucharist in its broad sacramental context in its chapter on "The Excellence of the Eucharist over the other Sacraments" (DS 1639) when it states, "To be sure, this is common to the Eucharist and to the other sacraments that it be 'the symbol of a sacred thing and the visible form of invisible grace.' . . ." Vatican II enlarged on this statement in the *Constitution on the Sacred Liturgy* in its description of the presence of Christ in the liturgy in general, stressing His presence in the Mass in the person of the minister and His special presence in the Eucharistic Species, His presence as the principal agent in every sacramental action, His presence in the reading and preach-

7. *De Veritate,* q. 27, a. 4, ad 13.

8. *Christus, Sacrament van de Godsontmoeting,* p. 77. The translation in the English edition does not seem as strong as the original. It reads: "It is not of course as if the sign, as sign, could have an actual effect, but the other way about; the gift of grace comes in its own visibility; . . ." (p. 74). The original makes a stronger general statement of principle: ". . . ; the gift of grace entails its own visibility; . . ."

ing of the word, and, finally, His presence in every praying community. The council presented the underlying principle of this presence when it said that "in the liturgy full public worship is performed by the mystical body of Jesus Christ, that is, by the Head and His members" (art. 7). The council is speaking of the liturgy in general and envisions every type of liturgical celebration which constitutes the public worship of the Church. But it can be seen readily that what it says about the liturgy is true par excellence of the Eucharist. For apart from the explicit statement of the presence and function of Christ in the Mass, the council indicated other elements of liturgical action which are all present in the Eucharist. The Eucharist is, after all, a sacrament, and thus is principally an action of Christ. In the Eucharist, Christ is the one who proclaims the word of God. In the Eucharist, it is Christ who includes the praying community in His own timeless worship of the Father as He "associates the Church with Himself in the truly great work of giving perfect praise to God and making men holy" (art. 7). For although the Eucharist can be said to contain many "sacraments," the "sacrament of the word," the "sacrament of the real presence of Christ under the appearances of bread and wine," the "sacrament of communion with Christ," the "sacrament of the praying Church," these "sacraments" are all moments of one sacramental action which is the whole Eucharist. The "sacrament of the Eucharist" is not to be restricted to the moments of consecration and communion but includes the whole Eucharistic action from the entrance hymn to the dismissal and blessing. It is within this entire sacramental context that the consecration and communion take place, and it is within the totality of this context that the questions of "presence" and change must be understood.

The consideration of the Eucharist in its broad sacramental context is complicated, however, by the fact that such a consideration must take into account the diverse moments of the Eucharistic celebration and at the same time relate these moments to the central meaning and power of the Eucharist which makes of these moments one sacramental action. This cannot be done with much clarity, however, without separating these two dimensions of the sacrament. Thus, the individual moments of the Eucharist will be presented first, but the whole purpose of this analysis is the later synthesis in which these moments will be related to the one central meaning of the Eucharist which binds these moments into a sacramental unity. For although a sacrament is a sign-act, it must be kept in mind that a sign-act is such only because it contains a central unity of meaning and power. Thus, the visible, tangible realities which are seen to be signs are only seen as such to the extent that they are actually the bearers of meaning. And if the sign-act is one act, it is because the meaning-content of the act is one.

Beginning with the diverse moments of the celebration of the Eucharist, it should be noted that even the multivalent ritual of the Eucharist possesses a basic unity in the fact that the whole of the action is the worship of the Church. Granted that every sacrament is an act of worship in which the Church implores the grace of redemption from the Father in and through Christ, the Eucharist is *the* worship of the Church. Granted that every sacramental action is liturgy, the Eucharist is *the* liturgy. The Eastern Church has preserved this emphasis more clearly in its simply naming the Eucharist "The Divine Liturgy." The expression is finding a parallel in contemporary western expression of the Eucharist as "The Sacred Liturgy." For the Eucharist is, in an absolutely unique sense, *the* liturgy in the root sense of the word: *the* public worship of the Church. It is precisely in the Eucharist as public worship that the Church is known as a church among the churches. And although the public image of churches is wider than church buildings, the buildings which house the worshipping communities are, in fact, the first distinguishing characteristic which comes to mind when one speaks of different churches. And there is nothing wrong with this usage. For it is precisely in public worship that the unique individuality of the Church and the churches comes to its most effective expression. Public worship is, in other words, *the* sign of the Church as a church. It is the action in which the Church brings to expression her own reality as a community of worship and sanctification.

The mention of worship, of course, brings to mind the ceremonial in which the worship of a community or an individual is embodied. What must be kept in mind is the fact that this ceremonial is the symbolic clothing of something which goes beyond the time of ceremonial worship. For ceremonial worship is essentially a symbolic reality, expressing in word and gesture the totality of the religious life of the community or individual. At the heart of all the ritual is the presence of the community before God as it actually is. Public worship is a sign-act, the growth through self-expression of the community before God. This self-expression is declarative, but it is more. It is the self-giving of the community in an act which expresses its reality as a community to God, who is the creator of the community. It is in this self-giving through self-expression that the community is conscious of itself as a community and grows as a community in the experience. The whole posture of the community at worship, then, is the posture of the religious community and individuals within the community as they actually are before God. It is the posture of the creature acknowledging the gift of his own life and receiving that gift in religious union. This is what worship is meant to be. Of course, it is possible to lie, even in worship. Man can perform sign-acts which are false because they do not present his true interiority to the world and he can adopt a posture before God which is not his real posture. The parable of the Publican and the Pharisee (Lk 18:9–14) makes this point quite clearly. The sin of the Pharisee is more than that of boasting. It is the sin of standing before God in the posture of an equal who demands his just recompense for services rendered. And man can never truly take this posture. Granted the enormous gift which God has given man in Christ, man is still God's creature and stands before God in the posture of one who receives everything from God out of the absolutely free initiative of God's love. God owes man nothing. And this principle in the theology of grace brings out the existential content of worship.

Worship has been defined as "realizing God in human life."[9]

9. Schillebeeckx, *Christ the Sacrament of the Encounter with God*, pp. 28–32; see also "De zin van het mens-zijn van Jesus de Christus," in *Tijdschrift voor Theologie* 2 (1962), pp. 128–132.

What this means basically is that worship is man's very life which is lived from day to day as a creature of God. It means that man's life is lived in such a way that within the pattern of his freedom, God, man's creator, is the most real value which gives the deepest meaning to man's life, because God is continually giving man his own life in the deepest part of man's personal reality. To the extent that man feels himself alive, he feels that God is real in his life. Of course, this means that man's experience of God, like his experience of himself, follows that pattern of "peaks" and "valleys" which is the rhythm of consciousness. A. Maslow has described this in his analysis of "peak experiences" in human consciousness.[10]

The religious man is the man who experiences God in this same pattern and makes his own creaturehood and God's reality to him as Creator a real aspect of his decisions. In this way God is not simply real in a man's life as an alien "transcendent" reality. God rather becomes real in man's life as man becomes real to himself; transcendent, yes, but transcendent within man's life. God becomes real for man as man becomes real for himself. This whole existential project of letting God really be God for one's self is the basic reality of worship. For then and only then is God real for man. Then and only then does a man in reality adopt the posture of the creature.

This existential living worship, then, is the living content of the ritual in which man in community (or in private, for that matter) "worships" God. To the extent that it is true in man's life, man's worship is true. To the extent that it is false, man's worship is false. It is not the ritual form of worship which gives it value. It is the truth of that form as it incorporates the life of worship which is man's realization of his own creaturehood. Jesus makes His own the prophetic criticism which Isaiah voices against the empty ritual of those who "honor God with their lips, but their heart is far from me; in vain do they worship me. . . ." (Mk 7:6–7; Is 29:13).

This, then, is already a central unity which characterizes the

10. "Growth and Cognition," in *Toward a Psychology of Being,* Princeton, 1962, pp. 67–126.

Eucharist: it is the public worship of the Church, the act in which the Church gathers together before God in Christ, acknowledging the fact that her existence as God's people is God's own and constant gift. As true worship, it must express the daily life which the Church leads as a community to be true. And, at the same time, it is the action in which, precisely because it is the symbolic self-expression of the deepest reality of the Church (that she is one in Christ), the Church grows as Church. Parenthetically, one can wonder whether this fact is not at the root of the opposition one finds to renewal in the public worship of the Church. This renewal aims to accomplish far more than a change of forms. It is aimed at a renewal of the community of the Church precisely as a community. Its meaning is the nourishment of the very spirit of "being in the Church."[11] It means the growth of love between the members of the Church. It is a constant reminder that no one stands alone in the Church, that all are responsible to and for one another. And this certainly runs directly counter to what was once called "liberalism" and now is called "conservativism."

Within the unity of the Eucharist as the act of worship of the Church, however, there are three moments which are the shape of the ceremonial worship: prayer (and song), the reading and proclamation of the scripture, and the communion-sacrifice. The first of these, prayer and song, make up the act in which the community, following the command of Christ, "Ask and it shall be given to you" (Mt 7:7), petitions the gifts of God which

11. Paul VI, "Mysterium Fidei," in *AAS* 57 (1965), p. 772. The statement bears citation here.

> Thus it happens that the worship of the divine Eucharist greatly moves the soul to the cultivation of "social" love, in which we place the common good before private good, we undertake the cause of the community, the parish, the universal Church and extend charity to the whole world because we know that the members of Christ are everywhere.
>
> Therefore, venerable brothers, since the sacrament of the Eucharist is the sign and the cause of the unity of the mystical body of Christ and stirs up in those who cultivate it with fervent affection the "ecclesial" spirit, as it is called, never stop urging your faithful to learn to embrace the cause of the Church as their own as they approach the Eucharistic Mystery. . . ."

make the life of the Church to be what it is: unity, love, forgiveness of sins, faith and so on. It should be noted, however, that this is not simply private prayer nor is it the collective prayer of all the individuals in the community. This prayer is situated within the unity of a sacramental act and shares in the sacramental character of the action as a whole. It is the public prayer of the Church in which she does not simply sum up the total effort of the community present but in which she enters into conscious union with her heavenly Head, Christ the Lord, addressing her prayer to the Father through Christ, who lives and reigns with Him. Of course, this prayer, which is principally uttered as the prayer of Christ, is not effective in any magic fashion. The pause before the prayer of the day is a time in which the community is to enter as deeply as possible into this prayer, mindful of their own individual needs, the needs of those present at the Eucharist, the community of the Church as a whole. But the prayer of the Church is not simply aimed at being a résumé of these individual petitions. Rather, the Church stands in the concrete posture of worship before God, praying in and through Christ, whose function is to unite the Church to Himself in His unending intercession before God. This, then, is a sacramental prayer and in this context it can be seen to be the grace-gift of a prayer of which man is radically incapable of his own efforts. It is the timeless prayer of Christ, entering the life of the community in the tangible visibility of the official prayer of the Church. The power of such a prayer is obvious, but it does not deprive the concrete community of the Church of its human freedom and bring about what it seeks whether the community wants it or not. It demands the attitude of worship in the community for its full effectiveness. It demands of the worshipper that he stand before God in the community as a member of that community, conscious not only of his own needs but of the needs of the Church, be it the concrete community present at a given celebration of the Eucharist, the community of the parish as a whole, or the entire community of the Church. This is liturgical prayer, the public prayer of the Church; it is sacramental prayer, the prayer of Christ uttered to the Father in the visibility of the Church.

Of course, some prayers make these dimensions of the prayers of the Eucharist more evident than others. The rather sober piety of the early Roman liturgy reflects them with particular clarity. In the prayers of the Easter Vigil, for example, the pattern begins with a profession of faith which calls to mind the blessings of God: "*Deus qui* . . ." It places man before the historical action of God, the root of man's faith. Only then does the prayer pass to the petitioning of faith, hope, love and so on. There is an echo here of the Jewish blessings which celebrate the historical blessings which God has given his people, and seek His gifts in the faith which these blessings found. This simple and direct style of prayer has a ring of the directness of the situation in which man stands before God, conscious of the fact that everything is the historical gift of God's absolutely free initiative of love. One would hope that in the on-going restoration of the liturgy, some of the somewhat Pharisaical recollections of man's works before God will give way to the celebration of the wonders God has wrought among men. Granted that all of the "flaming charity," "burning zeal," "glorious sanctity" and "seraphic love" of the post-Renaissance saints is in fact the work which God brings about in men, it still has the ring of the Pharisee standing before God boasting of his fasting and tithing.

But the most important point to be kept in mind is that this sacramental prayer is the prayer of Christ. It is, in the bond of the Spirit, the prayer which He utters in the community. This is the deeper meaning of "For where two or three are gathered together 'in my name,' there I am in their midst" (Mt 18:20). For it is in this context—the context of the Church living in Christ—that "two or three are gathered together." As Matthew tells it, it is in this same context that whatever this gathering binds on earth is bound in heaven (18:18), and it is in this context—the context of the community of the Church at one with Christ—that their "agreement" will be infallibly accomplished by Christ's heavenly Father (18:19). It is not simply a matter of Christ's happening to be where men are gathered together out of love and devotion to Christ. It is rather a question of that "alienation" of earthly actions in the fact that Christ takes man's action up into

His own constant prayer before the Father. The content of this prayer is not simply the petitioning of any one man's needs. It includes this, to be sure. But before this prayer, man must stand in his ecclesial posture, dedicated to the life of the whole Church in faith, hope and love, striving to blot out from his own life whatever separates him from the life of the whole Church in a sincere love of all of Christ's members.

The second moment of Eucharistic worship centers around the gospel, not simply the "gospels" of the four evangelists, but the "good news" of salvation as God has spoken it to man in Christ. More than mere reading, this action is a proclamation before which man does not stand in a "take it or leave it" attitude. For this is, once again, a moment of the act of worship. Thus, far from simply "hearing" the gospel, the Church at worship "receives" the gospel, "stands" in the gospel and "is saved" by the gospel, if it holds fast to it (1 Cor 15:1–2). For the gospel is not simply a book filled with words, but is "the power of God" working "for the salvation of everyone who believes" (Rom 1:16). The Church stands before the gospel, then, in the attitude of worship, receiving from her Creator the word which is her life. For, once again, this is a moment of a sacramental worship, an act which the Church performs in conscious union with Christ. It is thus, in the words of Vatican II, "He Himself who speaks when the holy scriptures are read in the Church" (*Const. on Sac. Lit.*, art. 7). The Church, then, receives the gospel in faith, that is, in the absolute openness to the power of God and His word, which tolerates no barriers of human making. The gospel is the very power of God, manifested to man in Jesus Christ, and working man's salvation to the extent that man opens himself fully to its saving power. It has an objective, a "given" power which does not come from man's faith, but at the same time that power can only operate in man to the extent that man freely and fully opens his life to that power.

Hearing and receiving the gospel in the public worship of the Church, then, is an act of worship. And just as the prayer of the Church is a gift from God in Jesus Christ, the gospel is likewise a grace-gift, given in Jesus Christ for the life of the Church. And this in not true simply in the sense that the gospel contains the historical words and deeds of Jesus. It means that Christ, the Risen Lord, is really present both in the prayer of the Church and in the proclamation of the good news of salvation which was and still is given to the Church in Him. It is Christ Himself who speaks when the gospel is proclaimed, giving the way of salvation to the worshipping community, and this way of salvation is a way of worship; it is Himself, the way, the truth and the light.

Further, receiving the gospel within the celebration of the Eucharist is sacramental worship. It participates in the unity of meaning and power of the one Eucharist. It is, as has just been seen, a sign-act in which Christ, the primal grace and the primal sacrament, expresses His own salvific reality to the community in and through the cultic action of His body, the Church. It is, as has also been seen, the grace-gift of God in the reality of Christ rendered visible in the community in the celebration of the word of God. This word contains the reality it expresses, the good news of God's salvation in Christ. As a sacramental reality, then, which participates in the meaning and power of the sacrament of the Eucharist, the gospel has an objective power. The important implication of this is that both the preaching and listening Church must stand before the word of God in an attitude of serious responsibility. The word of God must be understood; it must be the object of deep reflection and prayerful study if it is to be what Christ says that it is: "The words I have spoken to you are spirit and life" (Jn 6:63). The word of God must be preached with that honesty which comes not only from deep study and prayer, but also from the realization of that word in the life of preacher and listener. Once again, it can be seen that the liturgical renewal, in its insistence on the place of the reading of and reflection on the word of God in the celebration of the Eucharist, envisions a renewal in the worship of the Church which looks beyond the mere change of liturgical forms to the life of worship which the Church is called to live outside of the Sunday liturgy. Vatican II is really looking toward a renewal in the life of the Church in every aspect which grows out of the very roots of the life of the Church in the celebration of the

Eucharist. For this is, above and beyond everything else, where the Church receives "spirit and life," becoming not only a "living being" but, in her union with Christ, a "life-giving spirit" (1 Cor 15:45).

If the Eucharist possesses what might be called a "horizontal unity" in the fact that it is the one act of worship of the Church, the third moment in the Eucharist, the communion-sacrifice, is the heart of the act of worship and thus the basic source of its horizontal unity, and at the same time the principle of the "vertical unity of the Eucharist" as an act which is the one action of Christ performed in and through the public worship of the Church. For the central reality of this moment and, through this moment, of the entire Eucharistic celebration is the body of Christ. It is in that body that there is given the central meaning and power of the Eucharist as a whole. Granting that the text-book theology of the Eucharist has focused too closely on the body of Christ and the mode of its presence in the Eucharist to the expense of the appreciation of the unity of the whole Eucharist as the public sacramental worship of the Church, this focus is not entirely out of order. For it is precisely in the body of Christ that the prayer of the Church, the gospel and the communion-sacrifice have their unity as a sacramental action.

Chapter Two has presented the biblical faith in the Eucharist, showing how the New Testament sees the centrality of Christ's body in the Eucharist as the root of the meaning and power of the Eucharist. It has been seen to be the Church's participation in the on-going cultic power of the Incarnate Word. This means that the apostolic Church, belonging to the constitutive phase of the deposit of faith, preached the meaning and power of the Eucharist in terms of Christ's transformation of the cultic meaning and power of Passover by realizing in His own body the fulfillment of the meaning and power of Passover in the sacrifice which He offered to God in our name and in our place. Christ, then, the unique mediator, indeed, in this context, the unique cultic mediator between God and man, is God's grace-gift of worship to the community of man. In the celebration of the

Eucharist, it is Christ's own sacrificial act which is offered to God by Christ, who associates His Church with Himself in this perfect act of worship. That sacrificial act took place in history, it is true, and is not something which can be renewed in such a way that it is present here and now. But as a personal action of the Son of God, that action does possess a timeless dimension which is real in the timeless existence of the Son. It is with this reality of the eternal high priest that the Church is associated in the action of the Eucharist, actualizing the priesthood which is hers by her unity with Christ's priesthood in the bond of the Spirit.

For all of this meaning and power, then, the reality of Christ's body and its presence in the Eucharist is absolutely central. This brings this discussion to the question of the contemporary writings on the Eucharist. These will be presented and analyzed in the next chapter. But this also raises another issue which sets this whole discussion on the Eucharist into the context of a far broader renewal in theological questioning. The problem of the body of Christ, after all, is not simply a sacramental problem. It is a christological problem, an ecclesiological problem and, indeed, an aspect of the broader problem of God itself which is so prominent in theological endeavor today. For there is only one body of Christ, the unique individuality of the Incarnate Word. It is this one unique individuality which (better: who) subsists at the "right hand of the Father," in the life and action of the Church and especially in the Eucharistic Species. And following the principle of theological intelligibility enunciated in Vatican I, theologians today are setting the question of the "real presence of Christ" against the background of the theology of the Trinity, the incarnation, the Church and her sacramental action in general. For only in this way can there be gained that "fruitful understanding" to which the council is alluding in its statement on the relation of reason to faith:

> But indeed, when reason, illuminated by faith, searches earnestly, piously and seriously for some understanding of mysteries, it attains this understanding with God's help, indeed a most fruitful understanding, from analogies with what it naturally knows, as well as from

the connection of mysteries with one another and with man's last end; but still reason is never rendered capable of contemplating mysteries as it does those things which are its own proper object. (DS 3016)

Accordingly, it seems proper to devote some discussion to the current discussion of the reality of the Risen Christ.

## *The Body of Christ: the Unity of the Eucharist*

There is no room here for a thorough presentation of current trends in christology, but its general character can be presented here to the extent that it effects the understanding of the reality of the body of Christ. Classical christologies have struggled with the problem of the unity of Christ, the problem of how two natures can subsist in one person. Under the burden of a strongly essentialistic and conceptualistic style of thinking and speaking, the problem of the unity of Christ became the problem of one plus one equalling not two but one. On the supposition (unconscious, it would seem) that "nature" is extrinsic to the reality of "person," the problem became that of determining what it is that is the principle of unity in Christ, the "formal constitutive of the hypostatic union." The very word "hypostatic union" itself conveys the meaning of two things being brought to a unity. It should be noted, of course, that the more existential style of St. Thomas Aquinas's thought rejected this approach. He never viewed the humanity of Jesus as a "depersonalized nature," but simply as the reality of the Son of God's being a man. The unity of Christ is seen in the fact that the Son of God manifests Himself in the humanity of Jesus, not outside of it.[12]

12. This presentation is drawn from the recent writings of Schillebeeckx, P. Schoonenberg, S.J., and A. Hulsbosch O.S.A. Schillebeeckx's articles: "De zin van het mens-zijn van Jesus de Christus," in *Tijdschrift voor Theologie,* pp. 127–172; "Het bewustzijnsleven van Christus," in *ibid.* 1 (1961), pp. 227–251 (with bibliography). Schoonenberg took up this discussion in a paper before the Dutch theological society, "De eenheid van Christus en de preëxistentie van de Zoon," in *Jaarboek: 1963/64* (van de Werkgenootschap van katholieke Theologen in Nederland), Hilversum, 1965, pp. 92–119. The *Tijdschrift voor Theologie* for autumn (no. 3) of 1966 published an essay of Hulsbosch, "Jesus Christus, gekend als mens, beleden als Zoon Gods" (pp. 250–273), followed by commentaries by Schillebeeckx, "De persoonlijke openbaringsgestalte van de Vader" (pp. 274–287), and Schoonenberg, "Christus zonder tweeheid?" (pp. 289–306).

The point of this current discussion is the abandonment of the idea of the "preëxistent" person of the Son of God, "possessing" a divine nature who subsequently assumes a distinct entity which is human nature. Thus, rather than speaking of a "hypostatic union," an expression which conveys the "one plus one" implication, the current discussion prefers to speak of the "hypostatic unity," an expression which aims at conveying the fact that in the one human subjectivity of the one man, Jesus, God reveals Himself personally. It is an attempt to rid theology of the dualism which has characterized christological discussions since the time of Origen. This trend, then, presents Jesus not in terms of a personal individuality like that of any other man, but in terms of His own unique personal reality: the perfect self-expression of the Father, united to the Father in the Spirit. Christ, then, is the human form in which God reveals Himself. He is man because God reveals himself in created reality and He is God because in Christ the Father is encountered. In Christ, the Spirit is also encountered in that the Spirit is God who, in His own self-revelation, begets the human form who is Jesus. All of this stresses the unique personal reality of Jesus in His absolutely inseparable union with the Father and the Spirit as the "image of the invisible God" (Col 1:15).

Against the background of this discussion, P. Schoonenberg, S. J., presented the readers of the Dutch Catholic paper *De Tijd* with an Easter reflection on the "Reality of the Risen One."[13] The reaction to this very brief article and Schoonenberg's replies were subsequently gathered together, along with a restatement of his position in the June, 1966, issue of the journal of the Higher Catechetical Institute at Nijmegen, *Verbum.*[14]

Schoonenberg states the primitive confession of the Resurrection in the words, "Jesus is alive, Jesus is Lord," or "God has revealed the living Jesus, God has made Him Lord over the confessing Church." The tone of the accounts of Jesus' appearances after the resurrection is basically cultic; the use of "Lord" to

13. "De Werkelijkheid van de Verrezene," in *De Tijd,* April 9, 1966.
14. "De Werkelijkheid van de Verrezene," in *Verbum* 33 (1966), pp. 242–268.

describe what the disciples see (Jn 20:20), their adoration (Mt 28:9, 17), their recognition of Him in the "breaking of bread" (Lk 24:35), are basically a believing confession that Jesus is the Lord and that they have been sent to bear witness to this. Thus, at the heart of the resurrection narratives of the gospels and of St. Paul is the fact that Jesus really lives, that He really is the Lord. But the question for Schoonenberg is what this "reality" means. For some, it means that there is, as a result of Jesus' being raised from the dead, an "ascertainable, objectifiable" reality somewhere which means that in the appearances after the resurrection, Jesus was seen by the disciples because His physical reality was "there to be seen" in the sense that it is a tangible, perceivable reality. For others, such a presence is not what is affirmed in the gospel. What is affirmed in the gospel is simply the fact that Jesus lives on in the faith of his disciples, that it is their faith which raised Him from the oblivion of death. This latter, of course, is the Bultmannian position and unacceptable. Schoonenberg's discussion rather centers around his encounter with the first position as the result of his statement that the gospels do not present the Risen Jesus as an objectifiable reality. Admitting that the gospel accounts are more detailed than the simple "He was seen . . ." of First Corinthians (15:3–8), he insists that "they never come down to a generally ascertainable, objectifiable presence. Rather, God gives Jesus to be seen, or He gives Himself to be seen. He never stands there to be looked at." It is not a question of Jesus' "returning" from the dead; it is rather a question of His pushing through the barrier of death to the fulfillment of His personal existence. It is thus that He is seen.

Of course, it can be objected (and A. L. van der Linden does object) that Jesus ate, offered His wounds to Thomas. But Schoonenberg points out that John indicates the intangible quality of the Risen Christ (20:17), and that the emphasis on eating in Luke 24:43 is one of true presence and fellowship rather than on an objectifiable presence. The meaning of the bodily resurrection and glorification of Jesus is rather to be seen in Paul's description of His resurrection as the image of our resurrection. It means that man (not just man's body) will rise imperishable, in glory, a "spiritual body" (not a "physical body"), bearing the image of the "man of heaven" who is a "life-giving spirit." Schoonenberg characterizes the Risen Jesus as existing in a "fully personalized body," in the fullness of what is meant by "body and soul" but freed from the duality of corporal historical existence.

Schoonenberg points out that in this present state of corporal time-bound existence, man cannot express himself perfectly precisely because of the duality of the body-soul condition. Man can only partially express himself through his body. The blush is a good example of man's lack of control over his own bodiliness as the organ of self-expression. It reveals what one would rather not have revealed. In the immortal state, however, this duality is lifted from man's existence and the body becomes the perfect organ of self-expression. It becomes the organ by which man can reveal himself in perfect freedom, in which man can, with utter freedom, give himself to be known. Thus, the appearances of the Risen Jesus should be seen as the sovereign acts in which He (with His Father) gives Himself to be known. And what is important is that He reveals and gives Himself by His freedom alone. We cannot, in our condition, "fix" Him in our gaze by objectification, by ascertaining or "noting" Him. He is not there to be looked at; He makes Himself bodily present in the act in which He gives Himself to the witnesses He has chosen (including Paul).

The difference between this understanding of the reality of the Risen Jesus and that of Bultmann is obvious. It is not a question of man's faith evoking the Lord Jesus in his recollection. Rather, it is a question of a unique power of self-giving and self-communication which actually belongs to the glorified Jesus. He is known because He really gives Himself to be known, but, at the same time, man has absolutely no control over the sovereign freedom with which Jesus gives Himself to be known. His bodiliness is not subject to our power to make things the object of our knowledge. He is not "out there" in this sense. The Risen Jesus is an objective reality, but it is not objectifiable. This is particularly clear in the vision of Paul on the road to Damascus. It was only to Paul that Jesus wished to reveal Himself, and consequently it was only Paul who knew of His presence (Acts 9:3–9; 22:4–16; 26:9–18).

Schoonenberg brings out another aspect of the bodily reality of the glorified Jesus in his treatment of the meaning of Jesus' "living on" after death. He points out that when we speak of "living on" or being in the "hereafter," we are speaking of something of which we have no direct experience. We put the words in quotation marks to indicate that we are speaking in positive language of something which is really a negative affirmation. The "hereafter," after all, is not a thing toward which one is moving. Nor is it really the "hereafter," because it is, in a sense, already present in the personal reality which endures beyond the fact of death. The person who dies is no longer in time. He does not simply "continue to exist" endlessly in the way he exists before death, but comes to exist in a completely new way. Freed of the limitations of this time- and space-bound life, the glorified person can participate in the life of those who are living now in a way analogous to the omnipresence of God.

Traditional scholastic definitions of the person emphasize two aspects of the person: intellectual nature and incommunicability. Contemporary thought would modify this definition, however, because, as has been seen, communicability and the actual communication and sharing of one's personal life is of the very essence of being-a-person. It is true that this self-communication and participation takes place without the alienation of personal reality. One does not lose one's individual reality in the sharing. But, on the other hand, it is only by sharing one's self that one becomes a real person. And this personal reality does not cease with death. Rather, it is freed from its space- and time-bound limitations, so that the glorified personality comes to participate in the lives of others in a new way. Schoonenberg does not elaborate the modalities of this new kind of participation, but that is not the point at issue. What is at issue is the glorified person of the Risen Jesus. Man's life is a matter of realizing the intentionalities which are so essential to the human situation, but the human life of Jesus has an intentionality which transcends the human in the fact that His life is "for men" in a unique sense. For He is the one mediator in whose life God's own life is really given to man. Of course, the mediator of that life is the Spirit, one and the same person living and functioning in Jesus and in the Church. But the function of the Spirit does bring about a reality in the bodily existence of the Risen Jesus. It brings about a capacity to participate in man's life by literally sharing His own life with man. Schoonenberg points out that, apart from the Eucharistic texts, the "body of Christ" in Pauline theology means the Church. Is this merely an image? Theologians of a more traditional cast of thought would tend to say that it is, but scripture scholars and contemporary theologians are insisting that this language be taken seriously indeed.[15] Bishop Robinson sums up the feelings of many when he says, "One would wish with all one's heart that the non-biblical and deceptive expression of the 'mystical' body had never been invented."[16] Schoonenberg points out that this is, after all, a medieval expression. H. de Lubac's masterful historical study shows how this expression, which originally meant the bodily reality of Christ in the Eucharist, unfortunately came to be applied to the Church.[17]

Schoonenberg, then, insists that, as the "body" being that bit of world in which the person exists, the body of Christ is comprised both of His glorified individuality and the Church which is one with Him in the Spirit. This is the one reality in which the glorified Jesus lives. This does not mean, however, that Jesus coincides personally with the Church or that His personal reality is absorbed by the Church. What it does mean is that in His glorified existence, Jesus is sovereign and free over against His body and at the same time more closely bound to and identified with it than we are with our own bodies. In human life, the human person is opposed to his body, but is, at the same time,

15. For a discussion of the confrontation of two attitudes, see J. Havet's presentation of the Cerfaux-Zapelena controversy in "La doctrine paulinienne du 'corps du Christ': essai de mise en point," in *Littérature et théologie pauliniennes,* Louvain, 1960, pp. 185–216.

16. John A. T. Robinson, *The Body. A Study in Pauline Theology,* Naperville and London, 1957, pp. 51–52.

17. *Corpus Mysticum. L'Eucharistie et l'Eglise au Moyen-Age,* Paris, 1949 (2nd revised and enlarged edition).

completely identified with his body. Thus, the human person is his body, but, at the same time, manipulates his body in freedom. In the state of glorified existence, the freedom with which one transcends the reality of one's body is complete and, at the same time, the immanence and identity of the person with one's body is also complete in the way which has been seen (p. 105). In this same way, although in utter transcendence, Jesus is sovereignly free over against the Church, but He is, at the same time, more intimately bound to the Church than the human person is to his own body. Schoonenberg suggests that the basis of this theology of the body of Christ could well be the husband-wife relationship expressed in *Ephesians* 5:22–23: "For the husband is the head of the wife as Christ is the head of the Church, His body, and is Himself its saviour." The "great mystery" to which Paul refers in verse 32 is the fact that Christ and His Church are "one flesh" in the way that husband and wife are in the meaning of marriage as it came from God's hand at the beginning. The "mystery which is great" is the fact that the duality between Christ and Church is only apparent in their unity and in this context, the transcendence of Christ comes to the fore.

It is this one body of Christ which is the central meaning and power of the Eucharist. It has been seen that the Eucharist is a sacramental unity in its character as the public worship of the Church. Its prayer is the prayer which the Church utters in Christ and which Christ utters in the Church. Its proclamation of the gospel is a cultic proclamation in which the Church receives her very life in receiving the gospel. And the presentation of the biblical faith has shown how the communion-sacrifice is such only because the body of Christ is at its heart. For it is in the bodily reality of the risen Jesus that authentic worship has been given to man once and for all by God. It is in this body that the Church prays and in this body that the Church proclaims the way which is her life and light. It is all one sacramental reality in the bodily reality of the Risen Jesus. And it cannot be emphasized too strongly that the bodily reality of the Lord Jesus is one. Jesus does not have a "private" body and a "corporate" body and a "Eucharistic" body. There is one and only one bodily reality of the Lord which is one in all of these. "For there is one God and there is one mediator between God and men, the man Christ Jesus . . ." (1 Tim 2:5).

Thus, though Schoonenberg leaves the Eucharistic texts of St. Paul out of consideration when he speaks of the body of Christ, it should be noted that even in the Eucharistic texts the oneness of Christ and Church is present, indeed is the principal emphasis. Chapter 11 of *First Corinthians* certainly presents this strongly. The whole reason for the presentation of the reality of Christ's bodily presence in the Eucharist is the fact that Corinthians are ignoring this. But their ignorance is not in a lack of belief in Christ's presence. It is rather in the fact that this body of Christ does not bind them together as a Church. For some are hungry while others are drunk. This is no "Lord's Supper"; it is just a meal where some are filled while others go hungry. It is the divisions among the Corinthians which make their eating and drinking of the bread and cup "unworthy." In their divisions, they are profaning the body and blood of the Lord. And thus, if anyone eats and drinks without "discerning the body," he is eating and drinking his own judgment, because he does not discern the body of Christ which is gathered for the Eucharist. He fails to discern that the whole meaning of this action is the oneness of the Church in the body and blood, in the bread and cup. Thus he drinks God's judgment, visible to them in the sick who are not cared for, the weak who are not assisted, even in those who have died as the result of the community's neglect.

When it is said, then, that the body of Christ is the central meaning, and therefore the central power, of the Eucharist, it must be kept in mind that it is the one body of Christ which is in question. It is the glorified humanity of Christ in which the Church has the grace-gift of worship through communion in His perennial sacrificial reality. But this sacrificial body of Christ is not an objectifiable reality which we can see, touch and effect. It is present only because Christ gives Himself to be received, because God gives Christ as the vehicle of authentic worship.

And for this reason, one can understand St. Thomas's skepticism about the Eucharistic "miracles" which were so popular during the middle ages. Whatever their value be to demonstrate the real presence of Christ, these objectifiable realities are not the body and blood of Christ (III, q. 76, a. 8). Indeed, he insists that not even the eyes of the saints in heaven can see Christ in the Eucharist (*ibid.,* a. 7).

Further, the one body of Christ which is the central meaning and power of the Eucharist is inseparably united to the Church. The mind which seeks clarity of distinction in this matter will dismiss Augustine's explanation of what the body of Christ means: "You are the body of Christ." But in reply it can only be stated repeatedly that there is only one body of Christ: the fullness of the body in which the Risen Jesus subsists, and this body is characterized by intimate union with the Church.

Thus, the central meaning of the Eucharist, and therefore the central power of the Eucharist, can be expressed as "the Church at worship in Christ" or "Christ at worship in the Church." The effect of the sacrament is primarily the unity of the Church itself. Granted the other effects of the sacrament, their unity can only be seen in the central reality of the body of Christ. All the grace-gifts of the Eucharist are one in the fact that the Eucharist is God's gift of ecclesial worship in Christ, unity in the life of worship which one leads in Christ from day to day, unity in the authentic expression of this worship in the cultic, sacrificial, priestly reality of the whole body of Christ.

It is against this background, then, viz., that of the total sacramental reality of the Eucharist, that one can approach the current discussions on the real presence of Christ and the change which takes place in the consecration.

CHAPTER FOUR

# THE REAL PRESENCE AND "TRANSSIGNIFICATION"

THE theological literature which has produced the current ferment in the theology of the Eucharist is quite extensive, going back almost twenty years to the controversy between F. Selvaggi, S.J., of the Gregorian University and now-Archbishop Carlo Colombo of the pontifical seminary of Milan. The context of that debate was the relationship between theology and contemporary physical sciences. Selvaggi had approached the question of transsubstantiation from the point of view of a scholastic cosmology which made use of the contemporary scientific understanding of "substance" and treated transsubstantiation in terms of the change of molecules, electrons, ions, etc. Colombo replied that the statement of the dogma of transsubstantiation is not tied to any particular scientific theory, but is basically a theological datum, and should be understood in the light of the tradition of the Church. The debate is interesting, if somewhat involved, but it has little direct influence on the body of writing which led to the encyclical "Mysterium Fidei." For this reason, it will not be treated here. The reader is referred to C. Vollert's presentation of it.[1]

Parallel to the Selvaggi-Colombo debate, however, another stream of writings emerged which was more specifically religious and theological in tone. It is this stream which has led to the development of new language in the theology of the Eucharist,

1. "Current Theology: The Eucharist: Controversy on Transsubstantiation," in *Theological Studies* 22 (1961), pp. 391–425.

and it is this stream which will be the principal focus of interest in these pages. The procedure will be to present the developments in the literature and then to present some reflections on its merits and demerits synthetically arranged under the headings of "real presence" and "Eucharistic change." The most startling (and well-publicized) developments in this whole question have been in the Dutch and Flemish journals, and, accordingly, those writings will form the bulk of this presentation.[2]

### *The Developments in the Theology of the Eucharist*

The period after the second World War was, as is well known, a time of intense ecumenical developments. It was in the light of these developments that F. Leenhardt's pamphlet *Ceci est mon corps,* appearing in 1955, aroused considerable interest among Catholic theologians.[3] The essay is frankly written from an ecumenical point of view. Deploring both the Protestant fears of "Romanization" and the Catholic posture of "blind obedience," he offers the essay in the hope that both Churches will triumph over their own weaknesses and converge on the true center, God. Leenhardt then proceeds to present a strongly realistic theology of the Eucharist, stressing the reality of the meaning of Jesus' words, "This is my body." Picking his way between the extreme Protestant position which attributes salvific power to the word of faith alone and the extreme Catholic position which tends to make the sacraments acts of magic, Leenhardt emphasizes that the creative word of Christ has a power to transform man's world by charging it with a new meaning. Thus, when Jesus says, "This is my body," He makes bread the instrument of His presence for those who know how to "go beyond the simple sensible reality." Thus, when Jesus says, "This is my body," the sensible reality of bread realizes His presence and renders it sensibly visible to His disciples. Leenhardt insists that "this bread remains bread; that is quite certain." But he states this in terms of physico-chemical

2. A selected bibliography, arranged in chronological order, is appended to this chapter. References to the literature in this survey will be given in terms of the numbered entries.

3. Bibliography, n. 1.

analysis, which "will continue to find in it the same elements." And, in this sense, he says that there is no "transmutation" of matter in it. "Christianity has always reacted against an interpretation of the words of Jesus which ends by saying that the bread is materially the body."

Leenhardt insists, however, that there is a real change in the reality of the bread. Though it be unchanged on the level of its material composition, it has become something else because, in its materiality, Jesus has chosen it to be the instrument of His presence. This, then, raises the question of "reality" itself. Leenhardt states that "the ultimate reality of things is not in themselves, not in what they convey to our senses, even when these are improved by the most intricate laboratory instruments." In order to apprehend the substance of reality, "it is necessary to have a knowledge in depth, attaining, beyond what things are, the why of their existence." And this kind of knowledge is only open to the believer, because only in its relationship to God's intention and man's condition is this ultimate reality seen. Thus, the one who sees reality as that which science can measure will simply consider the Eucharist impossible, but the man of faith will see in the words of Jesus the ultimate reality which God gives to this bread: the instrument of the real presence of Christ to the disciple. This is what the word "transsubstantiation" expresses, then: (1) the substance of things is not in their empirical data, but in the will of God who upholds them; and (2) Jesus Christ sovereignly declares the bread should be His body, thus transforming the substance of the bread.

Thus, Leenhardt's Eucharistic realism is strong in the affirmation of the change of substance in the bread of the Eucharist. But he insists that "substance" does not mean the matter behind the form, the substratum of the accidents. It means "the final reality of things as faith recognizes it in God's creation and in His ordinance to His creatures." Further, in his ecumenical breadth, he sees no theoretical problem with the reservation of the Eucharist, and states the objectivity of Christ's presence in the context of the act of the Church. He has a great deal more to say, but these are the points which bear on the present consideration.

In the same year (1955) Jean de Baciocchi, S.M., published an article which, by placing the theology of the Eucharist in a more clearly biblical perspective, sought to develop a more carefully focused theology of the real presence and of transsubstantiation.[4] He presents the Eucharist as the prolongation of the sacramental value of the Jewish Passover, acknowledging his indebtedness to Leenhardt's earlier book.[5] The article is cast in terms of the historical developments of the theology of the Eucharist, showing how, from the traditional presentation of the sacrifice and sacrament following on the presentation of the questions of real presence and transsubstantiation, an evolution has taken place which situates these latter questions in the light of the former, reversing the order of treatment. In this context, the consideration of the real presence and transsubstantiation have been situated in a more balanced perspective; and in the current edition of the French catechism, the language has finally come to be greatly simplified by leaving the term "transsubstantiation" out of the treatment of the Eucharist. The reason for this is the evolution which has taken place in the understanding of the term "substance," a term which has come to mean a material reality with a certain homogeneity, with certain sensible characteristics. Accordingly, de Baciocchi sets out to restate the dogmatic idea which is expressed in "substance" and consequently in "transsubstantiation."

De Baciocchi eliminates the Lockean thesis that substance is a hidden substratum under a superstructure of appearances, with the implication that a change of substance can take place by the mere elimination of one substance and the replacement of it by another while the appearances remain the same or by the fact that one substance can come to coexist with another under the same set of appearances. He also eliminates the Humean phenomenalism which would see substance simply as a collection of impressions and observations and would see the sacrament of the Eucharist as an event in which the taste, color, texture of bread are somehow absorbed into the broader religious experience of

4. Bibliography, n. 2.
5. *Le sacrement de la Sainte Cène*, Paris, 1948.

the salutary presence of Christ to faith. Against the empiricism of Locke, he states that substance is the reality which is known by the mind from appearances and against the phenomenalism of Hume, he insists that the mind, much less brute experience, does not exhaust the substance of reality. He insists that God gives His gifts to men in signs, inviting man to deepen his own experience by a deeper penetration into reality, a penetration which includes the knowledge of God's own presence and the orientation He gives to man's life.

De Baciocchi points out, however, that the greatest sign and gift which God has given to man is Christ, the image of the totality of the Father. In Him, God gives men to know the deepest and supreme meaning of existence. God speaks to men as sovereign creator in the words of Jesus. But this Risen Jesus is the ultimate judge of the reality of the world. It will be what He says it is when He comes to judge and transform. Thus, it can be seen that things are what they are for Christ, and it is in the context of this relation of creatures to Jesus that the doctrine of transsubstantiation can be clarified.

As the Creator-Word, Jesus is the center of meaning and reality of all that is. Thus, as He gives the sacramental bread to the Church (a bread whose meaning and reality are for Him), He gives the Church His body, the one body of Christ, born of Mary, crucified and risen. Thus, though the empirical reality of the bread remain the same, the ultimate reality (substance) of the bread is changed in the fact that Jesus gives His body to the Church. This is basically the mystery of the universal and transfiguring Lordship of the glorious Christ. In giving new meaning to created things, Christ, on whose express will the ultimate reality rests, gives them new being. Thus, transsubstantiation and the real presence are not opposed to the symbolism of the sacraments, but rather are deeply rooted in it. And what is unique in the Eucharist (i.e., why there is no transsubstantiation in the other sacraments) is the fact that this sacrament signifies a complete gift of Christ, the gift of Himself to the Church. But such a power only belongs to an act of Christ, so that, even if Catholics and Protestants can both maintain that sacramental communion unites them with Christ's person, it is the specific of Catholic faith that Christ's gift of Himself is a gift of association with His sacrifice.

In 1956, A. Vanneste raised the question of "substance" and "transsubstantiation" again.[6] After tracing the development and influence of Aristotelian thought from Paschasius Radbert through St. Thomas, he grants that the meaning of the substance-accidents polarity does guarantee the essentials of Eucharistic belief: that the Eucharist is Christ and Christ alone, not Christ-and-bread, Christ-in-bread or any other type of combination. But Vanneste also calls attention to the fact that the scholastic teaching that Christ is present in the Eucharist "*per modum substantiae*" (in the manner that substance is present) is not, in the last analysis, far removed from the pneumatic presence of the glorified Christ, a manner of existing which is freed from being bound to the "accidents" of spatio-temporal location and situation. In any case, he insists, the fully developed theory of transsubstantiation is not the dogmatic statement of transsubstantiation. This is a determined theology of the Eucharist, not the teaching of the Church. It is an attempt to state a basically inexpressible religious fact in terms of human thought-forms. The full elaboration of an Aristotelian theory concerning transsubstantiation, then, remains basically on the level of a philosophy, on the level of what is known naturally. For the scholastic theology of transsubstantiation, what changes in the Eucharist is a principle-of-being in the reality of the bread, not the total reality of the bread itself. In opposition to this, Vanneste cites with agreement the work of Leenhardt, insisting that the deepest reality of what something is, is what it is for God.

Transsubstantiation, then, is a religious reality, not a natural phenomenon. Far from being a divine guarantee of the real distinction between substance and accidents in the Aristotelian world-view, it is a creative affirmation of what this bread means to God, and thus, of its deepest and ultimate reality. What transsubstantiation states ultimately is that it is not contradictory for bread to mean one thing for God and another for man. But

6. Bibliography, n. 3.

this is seen from the moment that one admits that bread is God's creation, that God, not man, gives reality its definitive meaning. Thus, when the Eucharist is brought down to its purely religious content, it can be seen that there is no special philosophy or cosmology presupposed, because the doctrine of the Eucharist does not appeal to anything that philosophy and cosmology find in reality. Transsubstantiation, then, treats of things in their deepest God-given sense, and any school of thought which treats of reality can be reconciled with it, whether the basic reality of things be called "substance," the "*en-soi*" (in itself), "noumenon" or whatever.

In 1958, the annual ecumenical conference at Chevetogne, Belgium, took up the question of the real presence, presenting conferences by Leenhardt, de Baciocchi,[7] Dom J. Dupont, O.S.B.,[8] and Dom G. Ghysens, O.S.B.[9] The conferences of Dupont and Ghysens stress the non-technical character of the Church's teaching on the Eucharist, viz., the fact that the Church speaks the language of the ordinary man, not the language of science or of a school of philosophy, except to the extent that these correspond to the common language of men of every age. Thus, the use of "substance" in the language of the Church is to be understood in terms of the basic and stable reality of things. The teaching on transsubstantiation is a way of expressing the real presence of Christ in the Eucharist. It does not add anything dogmatically to the scriptural accounts themselves, but stresses the realism of the Church's understanding of the scriptural presentation of the Eucharist.

De Baciocchi's conference reiterated many of the ideas presented in his article of 1955. Thus, he repeats his emphasis on the fact that the real presence is not an isolated reality, but must be seen in the context of Christ's gift of Himself to the Church: He is truly present in the Eucharist because this is truly the gift of Himself to the Church. But this gift is in a sign, the sign of bread and wine. Thus, He remains truly present as long as He remains

7. Bibliography, n. 7.
8. Bibliography, n. 5.
9. Bibliography, n. 8.

present in the gift given to the Church and in the sign of that giving, bread and wine. Once these signs change, Christ's presence ceases (the traditional teaching of "theological corruption"). He emphasizes the fact that this real change is the work of God's power manifest in history, therefore the work of the Holy Spirit, an important point of contact with the Orthodox.

In his presentation of the doctrine of transsubstantiation, however, de Baciocchi comes even closer to the writings of Leenhardt, in his strong emphasis on a christocentric view of the universe. He grants that the use of the word "substance" causes problems in today's highly technologized world. For the man of today, "substance" coincides largely with the scientific view of reality. It means an empirical reality with a certain homogeneity of structure and a certain stability of properties (physical and chemical). But this cannot be used in the understanding of the Eucharist, because it is precisely on the empirical level that nothing is changed in the Eucharist. There is no physical change; there is no chemical change. One can never discern the presence of Christ physically or chemically, not even with the electronic microscope. For the theologian, "substance" simply means one stable reality, seen on the level where the mind knows and affirms it. This, once again, raises the question of "reality": what is "real"; what is the ultimate reality which can be known in things? If one can only know the empirical, one can only discern the accidental; but if one defines the real in terms of its situation within the total context of all that is real, i.e., in the context of the totality of its characteristics and relations, taking account of a real hierarchy in these characteristics and relations, then Christ's action truly changes bread into His body, and what remains is the empirical, the phenomenal, the accidental.

> In the last analysis, it is a question of the scale of values: yes or no; is the world primarily through Christ and for Christ? If it is, the Lordship of Christ and its Eucharistic application cannot be an extrinsic, accidental application for any reality (p. 156).

In an *excursus* at the end of the conference as it appears in *Irenikon* (perhaps prompted by the objections of Charles Journet), de Baciocchi shows that such a strong christocentric view of reality does not do away with the distinction of natural and supernatural. The natural order orients man toward God. The supernatural order orients man toward the personal relation with God, Father, Son and Spirit, and concretely toward the Incarnate Word. Thus, reason cannot define natures in terms of Christ; this is the work of faith, but of faith in the real world as it concretely exists. And as it concretely exists, it is "through Christ and toward Christ" (Col 1:16).

Christ, then, as the center of created reality, is the ultimate meaning of reality. Reality is what Christ makes it to be. Thus, when Christ, the center and ultimate judge of what is real, says, "This is my body," what He says is true. To the one for whom empirical reality and physical science is the ultimate norm of what is real, this makes no sense. But for the believer, who sees Christ as the medium and center of creation, this is the true value of the real: what Christ says is His body is His body.

In the same ecumenical context, Max Thurian of the community of Taizé published his study on the Eucharist.[10] As can be seen from the title, the book strongly emphasizes the memorial character of the Eucharist, placing the questions of the theology of the Eucharist into this context. Thurian interprets the words "Do this for my remembrance" in the light of the interpretations of Jeremias and Leenhardt.[11] The Eucharist is a memorial, but not simply the recollection of a past event. It is a celebration commanded by God like the celebration-memorials of the Old Testament, the *zikkaron.* What is peculiar about these memorials is that God is present in them, renewing the covenant with His people as He established it in the great events of Israel's history. Every yearly celebration of these memorials formed a part of that history, renewing the covenant until it was to be fulfilled on the Day of Yahweh. Christ did not abolish this religious event, but brought it to a new level, the level of the new covenant given by God in Jesus. Thus, the Eucharist is the real "re-presentation" of the unique sacrifice which Christ accomplished once and for all.

10. Bibliography, n. 13.
11. See the interpretation of J. Jeremias, pp. 62–63 above.

The heavenly Lord offers Himself to the Church as the unique sacrificial reality. Thus, Christ renders His sacrificial reality sacramentally present in the Eucharist, so that the Church comes to participate in His ongoing prayer to the Father and thus offers herself to the Father in Christ and with Him.

Against this background, then, Thurian approaches the question of the real presence of Christ. He insists that this be not treated as an isolated reality. It is to be seen in close connection with the gift of sacrifice to the Church. But with that caution, he proceeds to state the theology of the real presence in the Tridentine terms: Christ is truly, really and objectively present in the Eucharist. This presence takes place in the Eucharistic prayer which is the memorial of Christ's death and resurrection. This is not, however, a localization of the glorified Jesus. Christ makes the host and chalice the place where He comes to meet His Church, and thus, the bread and wine become His "body and blood" (i.e., the whole Christ), though the chemical composition of the bread and wine remain. But this takes place in an action, for the Eucharist is not an object, but an action. Those present at the Eucharist meet Christ in the reception of the Eucharist, those at home meet Him and participate in the memorial when the Eucharist is brought to them at home. Further, after the celebration, Christ retains the relation which He established during the Eucharist to the species of bread and wine, so that He is truly adored in the reserved Eucharist. Thurian does not elaborate this presence of Christ in the reserved Eucharist with the same strength with which he elaborates it in the celebration itself. But he does state that the Eucharistic worship outside the Mass is the worship of Christ still "present" in the reserved species.

These treatments of the Eucharist all have in common an ecumenical background and intention. In April of 1965, however, a more specifically Catholic development entered the scene with the attempts of Catholic theologians to present the doctrine of the Eucharist in terms of more contemporary modes of thought and expression. H. Verbeek's study can be mentioned here.[12] He presents the Eucharist in the post-Kantian language of

12. Bibliography, n. 14.

*noumenon* and *phenomenon,* though not with Kantian intentions. Stressing the peculiar character of the bodily presence of the glorified Jesus, he states that the Eucharistic species, which are the phenomenon which does not really present the reality, are, nonetheless, the instruments which Christ uses to give Himself to the Church as her Head and Redeemer. Thus, through the consecration, Christ takes up the bread as the form of His manifestation, becoming substantially present. In this action, eternity breaks into time. It is not the question of one thing being taken away and another taking its place. It is a question of the earthly reality of bread being taken up into the timeless reality of Christ, who is truly, though not spatially, present there. This is an anticipation of the resurrection, when the material reality of man will come into an eternal way of being. What the species actually manifest now (the noumenon) is the gift of Christ to the Church: Himself as her Head. Thus it is the whole Christ who is present, Head and members, in the Eucharistic species.

Schoonenberg takes up the question of presence itself in a series of articles.[13] Previous studies, as has been seen, concentrated on the meaning of Trent's statements on substance and on the biblical faith which Trent presented. Schoonenberg approaches the question from a slightly different point of view. He presents a brief study for a phenomenology of presence itself, taking for his point of departure the human phenomenon of presence. Granting that a spatial contiguity has a great deal to do with the phenomenon of presence, he states that this is not of the essence of personal presence. Man has this in common with the animate and the inanimate, that spatial contiguity is the medium through which true personal presence comes into operation. But personal presence is not the result of mere spatial contiguity. It is rather the genuine mutuality of subjectivities in which two free, conscious subjects confront one another. The essence of personal presence, then, demands a free, self-determined self-communication on the one hand, and a spiritual openness on the other. There is only genuine personal communication when one person freely reveals himself (in material signs, of course) and

13. Bibliography, nn. 9, 10, 11.

another freely accepts that self-revelation in trust, in faith. And the faith in which one person accepts another's self-revelation is the product of a spiritual openness. To the extent that one person is "closed off" from another, the other is not fully present. Personal presence is a matter of mutual communication. It can be seen how this may well be incarnate in a spatial contiguity, but the reality far transcends the fact of being spatially near someone else. This is clear when one notes that even in separation one can be close to another. Thus, there can be an "objective" presence of one person to another in the fact that two people are in the same place. But when the presence of one is ignored or rejected by the other, there is no really full personal presence of one person to another.

Schoonenberg points out, then, that although a spatial presence is indivisible (one is there or one is not), personal presence allows of a richly varied range of degrees. And from this point of view, it can be seen that God can be present in a number of different ways. God is "present" to a stone, but God is far more present to the extent that He realizes Himself "to the outside" and *communicates* Himself to the works of His hand. Thus, God is more personally present to man the more He takes man up into the life of Father, Son and Spirit. But God is more personally present to man in Jesus than in any other self-manifestation. For Jesus is, personally, the self-manifestation of the Father, given to man in the participation of the one Spirit. Schoonenberg allows that this presence of God everywhere is common to Father, Son and Spirit, and is not the manner of presence which is peculiar to the Eucharist. At the same time, he wishes that the two, granted their distinction, could be considered in a closer unity with one another. Thus, the presence of God to the "graced" man is more personal than His presence to the man who is not justified. But this grace-presence is, concretely, in Christ and the bond of that Spirit who unites men to Christ. In faith, man takes Jesus to heart, the glorified Lord who is the source of salvation, together with the Father who is always with Him and the Spirit whom both give as their gift, the gift of oneness with God.

What is paradoxical about this presence of God in Christ, however, is the fact that it comes about precisely through a spatial absence. Jesus insisted that after His resurrection he had to go away. Only after He is gone can the Spirit, who is the real deepening of the faith of those who were with Him during His earthly life, come from the Father and Son. Only then is Jesus really "with" His disciples to the extent that they know Him as Lord. Thus, through the Spirit, Jesus is "present" to His disciples as Lord. Thus, only because Jesus is "at the right hand" of the Father is He present to His disciples as Lord. Thus, instead of asking, "Where is Jesus now?," it were better asked, "With whom is Jesus now?" And the answer to this question is, "He is with the Father now, and for this precise reason, He is with us to the end of time."

This presence of Christ to men here and now who accept him in faith is, of course, far more real and effective than that of a friend who sends a letter from far away. His word in the gospel is man's salvation. But of far greater importance is the fact that the sacraments are His actions, actions in which He is the principal agent, using the instrumentality of the ministers of His Church to render His action "present" in the community of the Church so that it is really Christ who baptizes when Peter baptizes, as Augustine says. These actions are sign-acts in which the Risen Jesus makes Himself present in the Church in the signs of the Church's worship. This is clearest in the Eucharist in which Christ is not simply "given" to the Church, but in which Christ gives Himself totally to the Church as the root of her unity.

Schoonenberg notes that, while scholasticism has always maintained that Christ is not spatially present in the Eucharist (*"illocaliter in loco"*), the considerations of Christ's presence have usually taken spatial presence as their point of departure. He notes the strong preference in scholasticism for the ontological and cosmological in the presentation of this mystery. In the absence of an appreciation of the meaning of personal presence and what is involved in the gift of one person to another, the scholastic approach has contributed to the mystique of the "prisoner of the tabernacle," the fear of biting the host, etc. But this approach fails to fulfill Trent's idea of "substantial presence," especially when it is noted that Christ's glorified bodily reality has no physical relationship to this world. It is not so many miles away, it has no effect on this world in terms of energy, rays, etc. That bodily reality is of a completely different order, that of the "new heaven and new earth."

Thus, an approach to the understanding of the real presence cannot depart from the mere concept of spatial presence. Ultimately, this kind of understanding would lead to the "impanation" theory which has been rejected by the teaching Church. Christ does not become bread. The point of departure must be the reality of personal presence. However, even this must be corrected. Schoonenberg has shown that personal presence, especially the first paradigm of such a presence in the persons of the Trinity, is a spiritual (though very "real") reality. It must be corrected, therefore, by the consideration that the Eucharistic presence of Jesus is a bodily presence. Recalling that personal bodily presence admits of numberless degrees of intensity and expression, he points out that the most intense example of personal bodily presence in our knowledge is the act of marital communion, a bodily action which is the deepest act of full personal communion in bodily signs. The liturgy often enough takes the Song of Songs as its communion hymn. But if the act of marital communion is looked at from the point of view of the depth and intensity of personal communion which it contains, some understanding of the personal bodily presence of Christ can be approached, —with the understanding, of course, that Christ's bodily presence transcends even this intense personal communion in a divine way. This transcendence can be seen in the fact that the bodily reality of the human person, though it be the organ of deep personal communion, is, at the same time, the principle of the separation of persons. This is not true of holy communion, when Christ gives His body in the Eucharist. In the Eucharist, Christ gives His bodily personal reality to be received under the form of food and drink, a form which suggests the most complete entrance of one personality into another and of the most unique oneness. In the Eucharist, Christ is given as one to many in the context of one meal. Of course, the mere act of eating or drinking does not bring about this intense personal communion. In common with the other sacraments, this bodily presence of Christ is an invitation, not an accomplished fact. Full communion demands full mutuality, and a man can refuse Christ, even in the Eucharist.

Thus, Schoonenberg situates the Eucharist within the personal presence of Christ to man as God, as God-man, as principal agent in every sacramental action. The Eucharistic presence of Christ is, in this context, Christ's most intense gift of His presence to the believer. For in this presence, Christ gives Himself, the gift of life to the Church (Jn 6:56 ff.).

Schoonenberg closes his consideration with a twofold caution. This manner of approaching the Eucharistic presence of Jesus is only useful to the extent that (1) the catechist sees this contained in the teaching of the Church, and (2) the students of the catechism are capable of understanding it. He suggests that this approach is not yet "theologically ripe" enough to be used generally and urges caution in its use.

Thus the ecumenical writings of Leenhardt, Thurian, de Baciocchi, Dupont, Ghysens and others began the discussion. In more Catholic circles, a fresh approach to the understanding of the meaning of Christ's presence appeared in the works of Verbeek and Schoonenberg. In the following year, 1960, there began the dialogue of criticism and reaction which has characterized the discussion since then. The *Collationes Brugenses et Gandavenses* published the reactions of O. Schelfhout[14] to Vanneste's article of 1956 back to back with Vanneste's own reply.[15] And in the same year, the association of Catholic theologians in the Netherlands took up the discussion of Thurian's book in a paper by J. Lescrauwaet, M.S.C., entitled "A New Reformation Study on the Eucharist as a Contribution toward Christian Reunion."[16]

Schelfhout, admitting his commitment to Thomistic philosophy, proposes that the heart of the Eucharistic mystery is in the

14. Bibliography, n. 16.
15. Bibliography, n. 17.
16. Bibliography, n. 15.

proper understanding of transsubstantiation. He sees an error in Vanneste's conviction that the Thomistic treatment of transsubstantiation is an open question. Schelfhout grants that Trent did not define the Thomistic position, but at the same time, he asks whether the "theological note" (the dogmatic qualification) of the Thomistic teaching does not take it out of the arena of free discussion. Admitting that the Thomistic doctrine is only terminologically present in the council, he sees in the explanations of the *Catechism* of the Council of Trent the fact that the council's use of this language was no accident and that consequently any explanation which departs from the Thomistic treatment cannot satisfy the council's position on transsubstantiation. The basis for this is that the Thomistic position is not an exclusively "Thomistic" vision, but is a reflection on the experience of every man. In this it coincides with the intention of the council. He concludes, therefore, that the council's explanation of the Eucharistic change proposes a doctrine which has a philosophical explanation in the Thomistic teaching on transsubstantiation, that the Thomistic position gives an interpretation to the language of the council, that the core of the Thomistic teaching does not belong to the arena of free questioning, and that, if not its form, at least its substance belongs to the authoritative teaching of the Church.

In reaction to Vanneste's contention that the traditional exposition of transsubstantiation, drawn from the terminology of the analysis of change, falls short of the mark in that it seeks to explain an essentially religious reality in profane concepts, Schelfhout insists that St. Thomas insisted that this change is a religious reality and its analogical character allows its application to the theology of the Eucharist. Further, he rejects Vanneste's use of Leenhardt's (and de Baciocchi's) christological view of reality, insisting that things simply are what they are—for God and for man. He rejects this as an ontological voluntarism which makes human knowledge radically impossible without knowing God's will and leads to nominalism. For the same reason, he rejects the statement that it is the creative word of Christ which changes bread into His body. Creation, he insists, is the act in which something is brought into existence out of absolutely nothing, but the Eucharistic change takes place beginning from a given object, a piece of bread. He cannot accept that the body of Christ is created in the Eucharist. He does not mean that this is Vanneste's position, but he finds the mixture of creation and change in Vanneste's work a basically voluntaristic approach, an approach which was once a great problem in the theology of the Eucharist, but which, thanks to the work done by the theologians of the 12th to the 14th centuries, has been eliminated in the Thomistic presentation of transsubstantiation.

Schelfhout insists that substance and accidents in the Thomistic synthesis are not things, but principles of being, known in metaphysics as transcendental relationships seen in reality. This has not been destroyed by the modern scientific endeavor; indeed, it has been strengthened, if anything. Further, he finds in Vanneste's position a return to the nominalism of Ockham, not the purely evangelical faith which it is proposed to be.

Vanneste undertakes a reply to Schelfhout as well as to the remarks which J. Coppens directed against him and Leenhardt, among others.[17] Vanneste replies that his article was an attempt to make a contribution to the literature which rose out of the Chevetogne conference. He insists that in all this literature no one has really attacked the problem at its roots (*gründlich*) which is the relation between the evolution of theology and the statements of the teaching Church. He traces the evolution of problems and language to the inclusion of the neologism "transsubstantiation" in the oath of the IVth Lateran Council in 1215. The point of the Council of Trent, then, is not so much the sanctioning of a mere word as defense of the theological tradition of the Church and its legitimacy. In its defense of orthodox doctrine and the language in which that doctrine is phrased, the council adopted the theological language of the day, as was its right.

The question of the value of the *Catechism* of the Council of Trent is answered by showing that, although it has the approval

17. J. Coppens, "Miscelléanes bibliques, xxiv. Mysterium Fidei," in *Ephemerides Theologicae Lovanienses* 33 (1957), pp. 483–506.

of Popes and bishops, it is not a book which imposes itself on the faith of all Christians. It contains the teaching which is more common in the Church and is free from error, but to impose it as the standard of orthodox theology is to condemn theology to a hopeless stagnation. In any case, all that it would add to the council, even if it were any kind of normative interpretation of the council, is the mention of the term "accidents" in its treatment of the species of bread and wine.

With Benoit, Vanneste insists that the understanding of the real presence is a matter of the understanding of the totality of its scriptural context, not simply an exegesis of the words of institution. Thus, speculative theologians must compare their conclusions with the totality of that scriptural context. Theologians go astray when they begin with a particular philosophical system or even with "common sense." The truths of faith must be clarified from the totality of revelation. He notes that this is the way patristic theology proceeded, comparing the New Testament with the Old and finding in the Eucharist the fulfillment of all the Old Testament ritual and what it promised. With respect to the Old Testament, the Eucharist is the "truth" of which the Old Testament was the "figure" or "shadow." But at the same time, union with Christ in the Eucharist is but the "figure" and "shadow" of what final union with the glorious Christ will be. It is this ambivalence in the patristic period which eventually gave rise to the problems of the 9th century and the exaggerated realism of so many theologians. Vanneste calls for this same kind of hermeneutic in the interpretation of the doctrine of the Council of Trent. Trent must be seen in the light of the whole of Christian tradition, not simply as an isolated event in the history of the Church. Men who interpret it simply in the light of one school or another can and have created the impression that transsubstantiation is just another kind of change, and not the unique change which the patristic period described as the action of Christ coming down from heaven. Patristic theology was far more faithful to the analogy of faith than was the later scholastic period.

Vanneste further asks by what right theologians simply identify the "substance and appearances" of Trent with the "substance and accidents" of Aristotle. He is irked when Schelfhout constantly appeals to the distinction between sense knowledge and intellectual knowledge when Vanneste is actually drawing a distinction between natural knowledge and the knowledge which faith gives of the ultimate meaning of things. To restrict God's action to the categories of human thought is to add something to revelation which is not there; and thus, in the realm of faith, this emerges as a hypothesis, and hardly as a datum of revelation. With regard to the accusation of intellectual voluntarism, he fails to see how the affirmation that things are what God ultimately wills them to be is in fact voluntarism.

But Vanneste brings out a deeper problem which he sees at the basis of Schelfhout's problems. Schelfhout had accused Vanneste of errors regarding the proper nature and value of real theological knowledge. In reply, Vanneste says that all theologians agree that knowledge of the things of God is always analogous, but what this analogy is is not a matter of agreement among theologians; they divide into schools. He suggests that a serious discussion on transsubstantiation would constitute a good opportunity to elaborate the meaning of such an analogy. Schelfhout had accused Vanneste of having too little regard for the living magisterium of the Church. In reply, Vanneste asks whether Schelfhout himself does not ignore the origins of that living magisterium in his expositions of the Council of Trent. In any case, the living magisterium of the Church is not an independent norm for faith. The one source for theology is the living revelation of God, contained in scripture and in the tradition of the Church.

In the meeting of the Catholic theologians in Holland in 1962, S. Trooster, S.J., presented all the developments both in Catholic and Protestant theology, taking note of the Protestant theological efforts which aim at eventual intercommunion and the current Catholic discussions of real presence and transsubstantiation.[18] The various attempts at a consensus concerning the Eucharist are of great interest, but not at issue here. In the course

18. Bibliography, n. 18.

of tracing the developments in current Catholic theology, however, Trooster laments the fact that although everyone confesses the real presence and transsubstantiation, the consideration of these aspects of the theology of the Eucharist is too often treated as a "cosmological miracle" and isolated from its proper context: the salvific sacramental event of the Eucharist as a whole. In regard to the attempts to reinterpret the traditional expression of the faith of the Church, he deplores the fact and danger of falling into the same isolated perspective and losing a great deal of the riches of the theology of the Eucharist. He notes with particular approval the work of Verbeek, and concludes with the hope that the renewal in the Protestant theology of the Eucharist will serve, as it has done partially, to renew the Catholic theology and eventually to reunite the churches.

Of particular interest are the remarks of Edward Schillebeeckx, O.P., in the discussion which followed Trooster's paper. He points out several matters of fact which are useful. The expression "*per modum substantiae*" which scholastic theology has used to describe the presence of Christ in the Eucharist, indicating that Christ's presence is not known by "accidents" such as shape, size, etc., is often misunderstood. All this expression actually means is that Christ is present, but present in an extraordinary way, indeed in a "spiritual way" as opposed to the corporal presence which people ordinarily experience. Thus, after the consecration, what was bread and ordinarily present is now Christ present in a unique way. But all this takes place within the symbolic reality of the sacramental act. The change which takes place is not physical; physically, nothing is changed. But the reality which was bread is now the substantial sign of the presence of Christ; it is Christ, manifesting Himself to the community under the appearances of bread and wine. That there is no physical change in the consecration means that the agglomerate which is known as bread is still known, as a physical reality, as bread. In opposition to this, Schillebeeckx proposes an "ontic" change—the reality of the bread is changed because it becomes a sign of Christ's presence. This is a substantial change because the bread is changed now into the substantial sign of Christ's presence. Thus, the Eucharist is different from the other sacraments in which a material sign is used in that the bread, unlike water and oil, is not simply an "accidental" sign in its momentary use. Here, the very reality of the bread is changed permanently into the bodily reality of Christ.

Schillebeeckx has no problems with the language of the Council of Trent, the expression of a change in substance while the appearances remain. He only has difficulty with the term "substance" if one equates the council's use with the substance-accident categories of the scholastics. He points out that, in scholastic language, when substance changes, accidents change, too. He would prefer to say that in the consecration the bread remains, but not the "bread-reality." He finds the language of Verbeek (noumenon-phenomenon in place of substance and species) too Kantian. He finds the idea of "transfinalization" as it is presented in the writings of Leenhardt, de Baciocchi and Vanneste too functional and not fully thought out. He sees, however, that, if this idea is developed metaphysically, it has real possibilities as a vehicle of expressing the Eucharistic faith.

On December 4, 1963, the *Constitution on the Sacred Liturgy* of the Second Vatican Council was promulgated, the first accomplishment of the council in terms of official documents. It is interesting to note how the council frames the "real presence":

> To accomplish so great a work, Christ is *always* present in His Church, *especially* in her liturgical celebrations. He is present in the sacrifice of the Mass, not only in the person of His minister, "the same one now offering, through the ministry of priests, who formerly offered Himself on the cross" [DS 1743], but especially under the Eucharistic species. By His power, He is present in the sacraments, so that when a man baptizes, it is Christ Himself who baptizes. He is present in His word, since it is He Himself who speaks when the holy scriptures are read in the Church. He is present, finally, when the Church prays and sings, for He promised: "Where two or three are gathered together for my sake, there I am in the midst of them" (Mt 18:20).

The council thus situates the presence of Christ in the Eucharist in the context of a wider appreciation of the real presence of Christ to the Church in all the actions in which she continues His saving work. This broader statement of the reality of Christ's presence is the fruit of the theological progress which had been made both in Catholic theological ferment and in the ecumenical discussions on the Eucharist. The question was not discussed in the journals to any great extent in 1962. Their efforts were largely devoted to discussions of the phenomenon and issues of the council itself. But following the promulgation of the constitution on the liturgy, the discussion began again. The theologians of Holland devoted a number of questioning studies to the question of the real presence. The catechetical journal *Verbum* published two articles by R. Sonnen, S.J.,[19] and Schoonenberg.[20] *Collectanea Mechliniensia* published a résumé of recent developments by P. de Haes.[21]

An earlier statement by G. Mulders, S.J.,[22] catechetical in its intent, points out from the beginning that any human language which speaks of God is very relative. He notes that today it is possible to see how, in the past, some modes of expression in theology have relied too strongly on human insight in speaking about God.

Speaking of "presence," Mulders takes his point of departure from the words of John: "He who eats my flesh and drinks my blood abides in me and I in him" (6:56). This is the presence of Christ to the communicant in the Eucharist. It is not a physical or biological reality, but a reality of faith. On the other hand, it is not right to speak of this "real presence" as "spiritual" if one means by that that it is "un-real" or as "symbolic" if one means by that "in reality not present." Likewise, the reality of transsubstantiation is not a physical or chemical reality. It is better expressed in terms of the faith of the Church than in terms of science. Thus, in terms of the 6th chapter of John's gospel, it should be stated as the bread on the altar's being completely removed from its normal human use and completely changed by Christ into the Bread which He is for us, given by the Father

19. "Transsubstantiatie," in *Verbum* 32 (1964), pp. 223–238.
20. Bibliography, n. 22.
21. Bibliography, n. 21.
22. "Eucharistie," in *Verbum* 23 (1965), pp. 122–129.

from heaven. To ask what happens physically, in whatever hidden way, to the bread is simply to ask the wrong question. It is a question of Christ's giving himself to us, to our faith. And this latter is explained by the fact that in transsubstantiation the bread comes to the full potential of its meaning in being taken up into the eternal action of Christ, "transfinalized" (Mulders does not use the word). He points out that the things of this earth only have a transitory substantial reality, which is aimed at the day when God will be "all in all" (1 Cor 15:28). The Eucharist is a foretaste of that moment in the fact that the bread on the altar is taken up into the eternal act of Christ and comes to participate in His fullness. Thus, this change is beyond physics and our material knowledge. Christ incorporates this bread into His own salvific reality and action and in this changes the deepest reality of the bread and the meaning of the eating of it.

The language of the Vatican Council and the ideas of Schoonenberg's article "Een terugblik— . . ."[23] are both in evidence in de Haes' article. He shows that although Trent stresses the presence of Christ in the Eucharist and that this presence has come to be called "the real presence," Trent did not take up everything. This raises the questions of the other "presences" of Christ: are these "real," and, if so, what is their interconnection?

Taking up the matter of "presence" itself, he develops it in the light of what Schoonenberg had written, bringing out the loneliness and lack of presence which is found so often in the most crowded of merely spatial presences. He exposes the personalistic idea of presence as that which comes into existence only through self-participation to the "outside." Noting that the German distinguishes between *"Körper"* and *"Leib,"* he points out that the former is the body as object, of a certain size, weight, shape and so on. But the latter sees the body as the means of personal communication, the expression of love, hate and friendship. In this context, de Haes points out that the scholastic idea of presence usually takes as its point of departure merely spatial presence, saying that the Eucharist does not involve this type of presence. Thus, the presence *"per modum substantiae"* which St.

23. Bibliography, n. 11.

Thomas uses to express the Eucharistic presence of Christ can be translated into terms of personal presence, the personal relation and communion in which Christ renders himself actively present to and gives himself to someone. However, de Haes points out, there is the danger here of "spiritualizing" personal presence. Some theologians do not see this as a "real presence," but see it only in terms of a subjectivism or symbolism. Thus, de Haes comes to explain the different modes of Christ's real presence and self-giving, modes which, he notes, are not disconnected from one another. Rather, they are merely phases of the great salvific reality when Christ will be fully present to man and "God will be all in all." The Eucharist is, after all, only the pledge of that future state of things, *"pignus futurae gloriae."*

De Haes then presents the reality of Christ's presence to the believer in faith, comparing this to the presence of an absent loved one. But the difference between this presence and Christ's presence is that He is not present to us in faith because faith "summons Him up," but rather because He loves man and gives man the gift of faith, giving Himself with the gift of faith. He presents the reality and power of Christ's presence in the word proclaimed in the gospel. And he finally presents the interconnection of the different modes of presence in the literal citation of Schoonenberg's article of 1959 (above, pp. 121–124). The presence of Christ is an aspect of the total reality of grace. It both precedes and follows on the Eucharistic presence. It is a presence in the believer, the worshipper, the worshipping community, the priest, the word of the gospel and, in this total context, in the Eucharistic species. This last presence of Christ, then, is no end in itself. It is rather the instrument in the sacramental action in which Christ gives Himself most intensely to the Church and to the communicant within the worshipping community in order to realize to its fullest the personal presence of God to man which is "grace."

Schoonenberg's article represents his "last word" to date on the subject. He feels that this presentation is demanded by the discussions among the faithful and especially among priests which he experienced during the clergy conferences of the diocese of 's-Hertogenbosch, which centered around the theology of the Eucharist. With St. Thomas, Schoonenberg says that the aim of faith is not toward propositions but toward realities, and specifically the salvific reality of the Risen Christ. Thus, the most important aspect of the reality of the Eucharist is not the formulation of the relation of Christ to the Eucharistic species, but the knowledge of the deep communion with Christ which takes place in the Eucharist. Thus, he proposes to analyse the reality of presence in its broadest aspects and thus come to some understanding of the presence of God in Christ before approaching the question of Christ's presence in the Eucharist.

In its most general sense, then, the meaning of presence is simply the fact of one reality being "by" or "with" (*aanwezigheid*) or "over against" (*tegenwoordigheid*) another reality. Thus, it implies a spatial contiguity of some sort, but a contiguity which has a meaning. Thus, books are present to one, but their presence is a possibility of learning their contents. Likewise, one can be both present and absent under different formalities, as any teacher or lecturer will find easy to understand. Further, contemporary personalist thought sees action as of the essence of real presence. This is true of the inanimate as well as of the personal presence. Between inanimate objects there is at least the action of physical pressure and influence. Without this interaction, mere spatial relationship to one another is a principle of absence and distinction rather than of presence and unity. Further, in the higher forms of existence (in personalist thought, the primary analogue of existence), the personal, this action is the action of communication. Schoonenberg points out that true presence does not precede this self-communication, but is rather brought into existence precisely in and by means of self-participation. He stresses the realities of "absence," "strangeness" and "loneliness" which are characteristic of the "lonely crowd."

Contrasting personal and spatial presence, Schoonenberg says that just as spatial presence consists of more than merely being in a place or point in space, that there must be a relativity to other bodily realities in the same locality (spatial presence, in other words, as distinct from merely "being in place"), so personal presence demands a personal relativity to other persons, not merely being where they are. Personal presence, further, demands more than "exchanging information," "passing time" about and with one another. It demands a real communication of one's personal interior. Not a report about one's reactions, but a sharing of them. This is a reflection of the role of knowledge in man. Man's deepest knowing function is not simply the putting together of concepts, but in the intuitive grasp of reality which defines one's personal relation and attitudes toward the real. Thus, genuinely personal presence (presence in a personal manner as distinct from merely being where other persons are) demands a free self-determination and a spiritual openness to one's world. Freedom is demanded for personal presence because one can only render one's self present to others by a free action of placing one's personal reality in the presence of others. Spiritual openness is demanded because genuinely personal presence is mutual. If one rejects the free action in which another reveals his personal reality, the other person is not really personally present; one is alone. The loneliness of the paranoid illustrates this. He cannot "read" other people because of his lack of capacity to relate to anything or anyone. Finally, Schoonenberg points out that personal presence is not static or indivisible reality. It is a growing reality which admits of many grades and degrees of realization.

In this context, Schoonenberg indicates that personal presence can be immediate (face-to-face) or mediate (the presence of a person through some sign of personal relationship. Signs or tokens of personal relationship are not as important in the consideration of face-to-face presence as they are in the consideration of the manner of presence of one who is absent. Such a presence can only be in a sign of the personal relationships between persons, letters, souvenirs, gifts and the like. Schoonenberg notes that their physical reality cannot bring about the reality of personal presence in any immediate sense. True, these things can render someone present in a mediate way, but this is only true to the extent that the personal relationship exists and that the character of that relationship is given to these media by the one who makes them the signs of his presence. Only by this existential fact do they acquire a new meaning, the meaning that they communicate a personal presence. In this sense, they can be said to be "transsubstantiated." Their physical reality remains; they are paper and words, jewels, shells or whatever. But they are not seen as such, because they are not given as such.

Moving to the more specific consideration of human presence, Schoonenberg says that it participates in both the spatial and the personal dimensions of presence. The earthly condition of the embodied person is an invitation to and the organ and vehicle of personal presence. Bodily relationship incarnates the reality of conscious and free self-communication. This all comes about in the context of a personal presence realized in spatial presence. However, personal presence outlasts, indeed is often enough deepened by, spatial absence. This absence often enough purifies the love of one person for another and thus deepens it. However, in the case of absence, personal relationship can only live on the hope of reunion, otherwise the proverb is true, "Out of sight, out of mind." This is true, however, in a very particular sense in the case of death. One lives in the hope of reunion, true. But the shape of that reunion is unique. Life after death, and particularly life after the resurrection, is not simply a continuation or resumption of the life which is known here and now. Then, God is "all in all" and human life and presence find a fulfillment which is different from the conditions which bind it in its present state. This is shown in the life of the Risen Jesus.

The life of Jesus is not a question of His spatial presence among men alone. Granted that Jesus was spatially present among men during His earthly life, that spatial presence was only of importance to the extent that it was the vehicle of the presence of the Son of God to those who believed in Him. In His glorification, Jesus' earthly limitations are taken away and His presence is as unlimited as His love. But even this omnipresence is only what it is meant to be when it is received in openness and love; otherwise, His presence is a judgment. Thus, though one might compare His presence to the presence of a loved one who is far away, Jesus is less present than the absent loved one because His existence is no longer framed in earthly dimensions, nor will it ever be. Further, His presence through His love is total and no part of Him is far from those who are the object of His love.

Finally, then, one can begin to approach the question of the presence of Christ in the Eucharist. However, even here, the consideration of the presence of Christ must begin from His presence in the community which celebrates the Eucharist, for He is present here even before there are any consecrated hosts present. The Eucharist begins with the "real presence" of Christ and aims at deepening that real presence. This deepening of a presence which is already real is the context in which one can approach some understanding of the presence of Christ in the bread and wine of the Eucharist. Thus, it is correct to refer to this presence in the species of bread and wine as a "real presence," but it is not correct to see this as the only or even the primary "real presence." His presence under the species is a fluid and transitory presence whose whole meaning and reality is directed toward a more permanent and abiding presence. This presence is by no means a repetition of His spatial presence as He was in Palestine; it is not a "condensed" presence which is limited to the dimensions of the host or the chalice. It is a personal presence of Christ who offers Himself to the believer.

It is true that one can compare, as many have done, this presence to that of the giver in the gift; but this presence far transcends such a presence. To begin with, no matter how great the love, the giver is not the gift, but here that is precisely true; Christ is the giver giving Himself. It is Himself He personally gives to the receiver in the Eucharist. And this is true of the actual celebration of the Eucharist and in the reserved Eucharist—it is the one Christ, giving Himself personally in order to deepen His presence.

This "realizing presence" of Christ takes place through the fact that bread and wine become signs of Him. Through the prayers of the community, bread and wine are designated as the signs of His presence. But this does not mean that Jesus is "called down from Heaven," nor does it mean that there is any physical change in the bread and wine. What happens is a change in the sign-reality of the bread and wine. For in the Eucharist, there is no question of bread and wine, but rather of bread and wine which already have a definite meaning within the sign-act of the sacrament as a whole. In this context, they come to take on a greater meaning, so that, without any change in their physical reality, they come to be the signs in which Christ gives Himself as food. Indeed, the moment that the bread ceases physically to be bread, Christ is no longer present. Thus, the transsubstantiation in the Eucharist takes place in a "transsignification," a "transfinalization," but this in the depth which Christ alone can reach in His most real gift of Himself.

The discussion continues through 1965 and 1966, but the literature is generally a résumé of what has been done. The years 1965–1966 produced a large enough body of writings. In March, 1965, H. J. Fortmann published a brief exposé in reply to many questions sent to the periodical *Theologie en Zielzorg.*[24] In April, Mulders published another synthesis in *Verbum.*[25] In May, S. Trooster, S.J., published his reflections on transsubstantiation in *Streven.*[26] In June, I. R. Sonnen, S.J., published another résumé in *Verbum.*[27]

In the spring issue of the *Tijdschrift voor Theologie,* Schillebeeckx began a series of two articles on the question of the real presence.[28] The first article is devoted to a painstaking hermeneutical reflection on the first two canons of Trent's decree on the Eucharist, the canons on the real presence and on transsubstantiation. The second article reviews the present state of the question in a presentation of the literature and proceeds to Schillebeeckx's own understanding of the present state of the question. The two articles deserve a presentation here.

Schillebeeckx begins by indicating a methodological error in some of the modern explanations of the theology of the Eucharist. This error lies in the fact that these writers undertake a phe-

24. Bibliography, n. 23.
25. Bibliography, n. 25.
26. Bibliography, n. 30.
27. Bibliography, n. 27.
28. Bibliography, nn. 28 and 34.

nomenological analysis of the real presence without asking themselves what Trent demands of us here and now. Just as it is theologically insufficient to stop at a mere historical presentation of what Trent said and did, it is likewise insufficient to propose a mere phenomenology of the real presence. One must ask himself what Trent means now and approach the *objective* meaning of Trent as a 20th-century believer. This means that one must understand the thought-forms of the men of Trent in order to understand the conciliar text. The mere material repetition of the statements of Trent at a time when thought-forms have changed so profoundly is dangerous. But, at the same time, the interpretation of Trent from our own thought-forms sells the work of the council short.

On the other hand, Schillebeeckx points out that the word of God is never found in a "pure state" divorced completely from time-conditioned modes of expression. And for this reason, it is misleading to refer to the decrees of Trent merely as a "clothing" for the real word of God. What we consider a time-bound thought-form today was, for the Fathers of Trent, a question of faith itself. The problem of the time-conditioned character of Trent's formulation of faith can only arise at a time when the thought-forms have changed. This means two things. First, it means that it is not possible to say that Trent was aware that its decrees were clothed in a time-conditioned language and thought-form. As long as a particular form of thinking perdures, it is impossible to distinguish it from the message of faith it conveys. And, second, it means that the contemporary problematic must be taken into account when one wished to investigate and state the faith of Trent to the present age of civilization. The mere repetition of the statements of Trent in a time when words have new meaning and connotations distorts the teaching of Trent.

Passing on to the hermeneutic reflection on the two canons in question, Schillebeeckx points out that the discussions in which the canons found their origin, refinement and final redaction indicate that the expressions "true", "real" and "substantial" describing the presence of Christ reinforce the statement of the reality of the presence of Christ in the Eucharist. A move by some theologians to substitute "accidents" for "species" in the second canon was rejected for the simple reason that "species" was already in the text and had a longer history in Catholic tradition. Finally, he points out that in the second canon on transsubstatiation the final form, to the effect that the Church "most aptly" calls this change "transsubstantiation," replaced earlier proposals which based this appellation on the tradition of the Fathers or on the use of the "universal Catholic Church."

Thus, there are three levels of affirmation in the statements contained in these two canons. First, there is the biblical faith of the Church in the real presence of Christ in the Eucharist, the central and basic affirmation of the *Eucharistic* real presence of Christ. Second, there is the statement that this Eucharistic presence cannot be affirmed without also affirming a change of the substance of the bread into the substance of the body of Christ, etc. Finally, there is the statement of the aptness of the name of this change: transsubstantiation.

Beginning with the last statement, Schillebeeckx indicates that, although there was no opposition to the statement of the substantial conversion of the bread and wine into Christ's body and blood, there were objections to the basis for and the very name of transsubstantiation. The name was defended as a legitimate tradition, albeit short, of the theology of the Church, just as the word "consubstantial" (*homoousios*) is a legitimate expression of the unity of substance of Father and Son in the Council of Nicea. Further, because of Luther's rejection of the term and its content, with the consequent character which the real presence took on in Lutheran faith, the term was proposed as a shibboleth of the specific belief of the Catholic Church in the unique manner of Christ's presence in the Eucharist. It is a banner of orthodoxy of Catholic faith in the Eucharist. Schillebeeckx points out that this is no longer true, since many Protestant theologians have recognized the value of the expression and have accepted it. It has thus lost its function of being the hallmark of orthodox belief in the Eucharist.

The first theological question at issue, however, is the connection between the affirmation of the real presence and the affirmation of the substantial change in the Eucharist. In the discussion preparing the text of the canons, Schillebeeckx sees both affirmations as reductively the same. Together, taken in the context of the times, they do not constitute two dogmas, but are the forceful statement of the real presence, no more and no less. But this still leaves the theological question of whether there is an *inner* theological connection between the two affirmations. From this point of view, Schillebeeckx points out, although both statements constitute the teaching Church's affirmation of the real presence, and although the treatment of the change is secondary to the statement of the fact of the real presence, they are so connected that the denial of the change is a denial of the reality of Christ's specifically Eucharistic presence as the Church has seen this. Further, since the medieval doctors, the interrelation of these two considerations has been a necessary one (Schillebeeckx cites Sts. Thomas and Bonaventure). Bonaventure appeals to the tradition of the Church, but St. Thomas sees it as a theological conclusion so necessary that the two affirmations simply involve each other. It is this theological conclusion which, in the mentality of the Fathers of Trent, became an affirmation of the faith of the Church. Thus, though the two considerations are reductively statements of the same fact of faith, they are so interrelated that the denial of the substantial conversion is tantamount to the denial of the specific Eucharistic presence of Christ which has been the faith of the Church. They are, in other words, not so closely interrelated that they are simply one statement. It is not enough simply to maintain the faith of the Church in the real presence while rejecting the Church's faith in the true substantial conversion which this presence demands.

But the affirmation of the radical substantial change of bread and wine into the body and blood of Christ can be made on two levels and this consideration raises the question of whether both these levels are present in the decrees of Trent. The council affirms the fact of a "substantial" (radical) change in the bread and wine. The question which arises is: Does this mean that the council also sanctions the Aristotelian philosophy in whose terms this change is stated? Schillebeeckx answers this affirmatively and negatively. He laments the fact that modern historians of Trent insist that the council consciously removed itself from Aristotle's philosophy of nature in its statements on the Eucharist. The reasons adduced for this claim are the fact that the council uses the expression "species" instead of "accidents" as the correlative of "substance," and second, the council's avowed disinterest in the intramural disputes between schools. Granted the validity of the second reason, Schillebeeckx insists that neither that nor the first (the use of "species" instead of "accidents") constitutes a conscious removal from an Aristotelian philosophy of nature. In connection with the use of the word "species" he points out that the discussions show that the two expressions were considered equivalent, that either version was acceptable (*"utraque lectio placet"*) and that the reason for the use of "species" is the mere fact that it was already "in possession" as part of the text and that the expression had a long history in the language of the Church. Further, he points out that, given the scholastic background of all of the Fathers of Trent, a conscious removal from the scholastic categories of the philosophy of nature would be tantamount to a bald refusal to reflect reasonably on the content of faith. These were the only thought-categories available to the men of that time, and to expect these men to remove themselves from them is simply asking too much of them. Finally, he indicates that to claim that Trent consciously removed itself from the only thought-forms available to it actually takes the ground out from under the claim that Trent saw its statements as time-conditioned. The reason for this is that if Trent did so, actually distinguishing its statements from the contemporary philosophy of nature, it follows that what Trent stated is *not* time-conditioned at all, but the timeless statement of the faith of the Church—and that therefore every age is bound to the very verbalization of Trent's decrees!

In actual fact, Schillebeeckx points out, Trent's use of Aristotelian thought-forms is already a "transsubstantiated" Aristotelianism. The case of John Wyclif indicates this clearly. Wyclif's adoption of Berengar's position on the merely symbolic presence of Christ in the Eucharist is, in fact, the result of his pure

Aristotelianism. His reason for his rejection of the real presence is precisely the fact that, in the pure Aristotelian philosophy of nature, substance and accidents are metaphysically inseparable. Thus the Council of Constance, in order to preserve the authentic faith of the Church, insisted that accidents can exist without substance. And Trent, bound to these same thought-forms, insisted that the faith of the Church in the Eucharist can only be expressed in terms of "transsubstantiation."

On the other hand, Schillebeeckx cannot accept E. Gutwenger's contention that Trent and Constance make the Aristotelian philosophy of nature the only acceptable thought-form for Catholic faith. Granted that, just as in St. Thomas, the level of faith (the particularity of Christ's Eucharistic presence), ontology (the radical conversion of the reality of the bread and wine—*"transentatio," "conversio totius entis"*), and the philosophy of nature (trans-substantiation) form one total vision of faith for Trent, the three levels of affirmation are distinct and do not necessarily involve one another. Thus, since the vision of faith does involve a vision of reality, the faith in the real presence does demand the consciousness of an ontological change in the bread and wine, but the philosophy of nature involved in this change is not necessarily involved in the ontological fact of the change. After all, the change on which Trent is insisting, is the same fact of change which has been the faith of the Church from the earliest time. Schillebeeckx adduces the names for this change which have been part of the tradition of the Church since the time of the Greek Fathers: transformation, transfusion, transmutation, transelementation, etc. These expressions affirm the same ontological fact of change, but without the Aristotelian philosophy of nature. For the Greek Fathers, things are what they are by the fact that they are possessed by "Powers." Thus, a change in the reality of what is comes about by its coming into the possession of another "Power." In the Eucharist this means that the realities of bread and wine come into the possession of Christ through the action of the Spirit. Christ takes possession of the apparent reality of bread and wine as His own body and blood. This is all an extension of the vision of the Incarnation so that instead of Christ's divine personality being present in the Eucharist "by concomitance" (*vi concomitantiae*), His divine presence is the primary accent in the thought of the Greek Fathers. This is a statement of a true "transsubstantiation," but not involving an Aristotelian philosophy of nature. It is this ontological fact which is at issue in the decrees of Trent.

All of this suggests, then, that the Tridentine canon on transsubstantiation presents a reality for our faith which need not be explained in terms of an Aristotelian philosophy of nature. What is affirmed is the reality of the change in the Eucharist, and the reality of this change, with or without the underpinnings of Aristotle's philosophy of nature, is the burden of the whole of tradition.

The final consideration of the first article is that of the "basic question" (*de grondvraag*), the "real problem" (*het eigenlijke probleem*) in every hermeneutical reflection: "What is *reality?*" Admitting to Leenhardt's statement that things are ultimately what they are for God, Schillebeeckx insists, however, that this view of reality still differs from the "Catholic" view of reality. Granted that God is the ultimate ground of all reality, he insists that Catholic reflection on reality cannot accept Leenhardt's "extrinsicism." Granted that things are what they are by the creative word of God, this word brings it about that things are what they are in an *absolute* and *interior* way. Thus, there is a clear disagreement between Leenhardt's ontology and that of the "Catholic" view of reality. Does this mean that there is also a difference of what is affirmed *in faith* concerning the Eucharist? Schillebeeckx insists that a difference in ontology is, in effect, a difference in faith. The affirmation of faith is, after all, an affirmation about reality in the sense that it possesses a certain ontological density because it expresses how the believer experiences his faith in a real world.

Thus, just as God's sovereignly free initiative is the root of every reality of grace, this initiative brings about a reality, indeed in the very "secular," worldly reality of man, a reality which Catholic theology designates by the name "created grace." In the case of the Eucharist, this *real* created effect means that the reality of bread cannot remain what it was. And it is this created effect of the creative action of God's word which is contained in the Tridentine expression "*conversio*" (change). The canon on transsubstantiation affirms explicitly the change which is implicitly contained in the canon on the real presence of Christ in the Eucharist. The point at issue in this question is that of how God comes to meet the believer in grace. Schillebeeckx insists that in this sacramental reality, God comes to meet the believer *in* earthly realities, not simply by a relationship which "by-passes" the earthly by a direct relationship between God and man. Thus, the "grace-ing" gift of God does not come directly to man from God by a relation which the bread has (and which man has) *directly* to God. Rather, God's gift of Christ in the Eucharist has an effect on the reality of the Eucharistic bread itself, so that God gives Christ precisely in and through a reality which is no longer simply bread in its ultimate reality. Only because of this ontological change can the bodily act of eating be a salvific action.

> For these reasons, transsubstantiation contains two dimensions: to be sure, a *change-of-being* of the bread and wine (in which the gift of Christ's glorified, life-giving body is really accomplished), but this *within* the *earthly but now* (because of the change-in-being) *sacramental form* of bread and wine which, in this wordly world, remain subject to the earthly laws of bodily realities (in this case: the sacramental form of this botanical cultural product which, in daily life, we eat as bread and drink as wine. (p. 170)

Schillebeeckx's second article undertakes an analysis of the contemporary writings and presents his own understanding of the Eucharistic presence of Christ. The times call for such a reinterpretation, he insists, because the simple verbal repetition of dogma in these times is both useless and irresponsible. Dogma must be reinterpreted both in order to be able to preserve the soundness of dogma itself and in order to give men of this age a new possibility of experiencing the truth of the Church's belief.

Schillebeeckx then proceeds to indicate five factors which have brought about the present attempts at reëvaluation of the traditional explanations of the Eucharistic dogma. The first is the conflict which has developed between the Aristotelian philosophy of nature and contemporary physics. The Kantian critique and other modern philosophical analyses called into question the existence of a reality "behind" the phenomenal world which is unseen but known as basic reality. Quantum physics made it impossible to maintain that material realities can be called substance, that is, that they possess an existential unity of being. Thus the concept of substance came to be applied only to man. The more philosophers and theologians attempted to incorporate this new understanding of the physical world into the theology of the Eucharist, the more apparent it became that the Eucharist has nothing to do with physical-chemical structures and sacramental physicism was overcome. Theologians came to see that an approach to the analysis of the Eucharist from the categories of an ontology of nature was intenable and passed over to the proper starting place for reinterpretation: the metaphysical and sacramental.

The second factor which contributed to the new approach was the rediscovery of the principle *"Sacramentum est in genere signi"* (the sacrament is in the category of "sign"). The reaction of Trent to the Reformation placed great emphasis on the sacraments as instruments of grace and the sign-value of the sacraments fell into obscurity. The reëmphasis on the sign-value and -function of the sacraments clarified the state of the question of the real presence. It became a question of situating the question of the presence within this (the Eucharistic) sign-action safeguarding, at the same time, the realism of the Tridentine dogma of transsubstantiation. Modern phenomenological thought contributed considerably to the solution of this problem. Rather than viewing the sign from a *gnoseological* point of departure (viz., that the sign is an indication of something which is an *absent* reality), phenomenological thought situates the reality of the sign in an *anthropology* of the symbolic action. The prime analogue of the sign is human corporality itself, *in* which (not "behind" which) the spiritual "interiority" of the human person effectively communicates itself to its world of persons and things. Thus, the human person is experienced directly in the symbolic action, and need not conclude to the reality of the person by some sort of deduction from the sign. This consideration of the sign-act removes the sacraments from the level of the reified, objectified or static realities and relocates them within the categories of interpersonal dynamics: the sacraments are personal "encounters" in which God and man reveal themselves effectively to one another, with all that this implies for the full realization of the reality of "grace."

The third factor leading to the new interpretations is the attempt to interpret what Trent means by the "substance of bread" from the point of view of the new world-view. The attempts ranged from the position that Trent and Constance make the Aristotelian philosophy of nature the necessary prelude to Catholic faith to the position that Trent consciously removed itself from any Aristotelian thought-form. The contact with the modern mind, above all the mind of Reformation theology, has forced a reinterpretation of the Tridentine idea of "substance."

The fourth factor is the restatement of the manifold "real presence of Christ" in the *Constitution on the Sacred Liturgy* of Vatican II. Granted that each "presence of Christ" in the liturgy has its own density, the "presences" are nonetheless real. All of these modes of presence are being analyzed in terms of their direction toward the union between Christ and the believer and among the members of the community in Christ. Thus, both the ancient Christian vision and Trent's *"ut sumatur institutum"* (instituted to be received) regain the fullness of their significance.

Fifth and finally, the ecumenical endeavor, with its vision of the genuineness of the ecclesial character of Protestant churches, has forced an evaluation of the Eucharistic experience of other Christian communities. Further, the Protestant reëvaluation of the Eucharist stressed the realism of the original reformation theology of the Eucharist before it fell under the "spiritualizing" influence of Zwingli.

After a résumé of the current literature on the theology of the Eucharist (most of which has already been presented), Schillebeeckx passes to his own synthesis of the question of the properly

Eucharistic real presence of Christ. Accepting the position that the Pauline account represents an older tradition than that of Mark, he indicates a dogmatic development in the appreciation of the Eucharist within the New Testament itself. Paul's treatment of the Eucharist emphasizes the fact that the primitive Christian community experienced itself as such, a community in Christ, the people of the new covenant, the eschatological community on its pilgrim way to God's kingdom. The Marcan treatment, however, already contains a more one-sided emphasis on the reality of the presence of Christ in the Eucharist. This emphasis placed the eschatological and communitarian emphasis in the context of the specifically cultic context of the presence of Christ as sacrificial. In this development, the real presence of Christ is set against the background of the eschatological communion with Christ who is now at work in His body, the Church. This is the way in which the apostolic Church experienced itself precisely as a Church. This emphasis, belonging as it does to the constitutive phase of revelation, is normative for the experience of the Church today. And this means that not only must the Church of today revere the witness of the apostolic Church, but it must also have the same reverence for the development of the experience of the Eucharist which has developed over the centuries under the inspiration and guarantee of the Spirit. The directing principle is the apostolic witness, it is true, but this witness can only be soundly interpreted today in terms of the thought-forms of this day and age in the life of the Church and of world in which it lives.

The basic principle of Schillebeeckx's synthesis is the fact that reality is not of man's making. In this light, he presents the "given-ness" of the Eucharist. Its broad context is that of "proclaiming the death of the Lord" in a meal which has been constituted as the sacramental memorial of the death, resurrection and glorification of Christ. Only in this context can one speak of the real presence in any significant way.

The development of the reality of "real presence" begins with a consideration of God's presence to man in creation. Given the fact of creation, God is the ultimate meaning and reality of the world for man. Of course, not every man knows this, only the believer can know it. But this ultimate reality and presence of God to man *in* created reality is a real, a metaphysical value of the world as it concretely is. The world, then, is a sign of God to man. For man this means that the deepest reality of the world is a mystery; it is the revelation of God to man. This basically mysterious world is the basis of man's life, a life in which man lives to find and give meaning to the world and to himself as a part of the world. The world, then, is the Creator's gift to man, and this "for-man" character of the world is the basis of his assignment of meaning to the world and to himself (on the basis of what the world *is in itself,* of course).

Applying these principles to the reality of bread, Schillebeeckx points out that bread is itself a cultural product of man, made by man because of the meaning he sees (a "given" meaning) in the biological realities which compose it. On this basis, bread takes on a variety of meanings for man: nourishment, the congeniality of the mealtime, the sealing of friendship, and so on. This does not eliminate the biological reality of bread, but assumes that reality into a higher level of meaning and function: a specifically *human* meaning and function. Thus, though bread remains bread physically, it is "transsignified," "humanized" (*vermenselijkt*). And this transsignification of the physical reality of bread is more than a mere relation; it is an "essential correlation between the object bread and the subject man within the mystery of the reality in which the world is given to us and we to one another."

What is important is this analysis is the fact that the world has different meanings for man (real meanings) on different levels. Thus, the description of reality from a human standpoint must determine the level on which it describes reality and remain on that level, not wandering from one level to another. From this point of view, then, the very question, "After the consecration, is this bread ordinary bread?", is meaningless for the simple reason that in the same question one wanders from the cultic to the physical level. One can ask the physical question, of course, but one cannot expect an answer to a question placed on the level which responds on the cultic, in this case, theological level. Schillebeeckx points out that this confusion of levels has troubled the theology of the Eucharist almost universally. A physical answer to a sacramental question can say something physical, it is true, but this answer is sacramentally (Eucharistically) irrelevant. And for this reason, one cannot look at the Eucharistic transsubstantiation outside the sphere of the assignment of meaning in sacramental signs. This question must be asked in the specifically *paschal* context of Christ's self-giving. This consideration does not answer the question of the identity or non-identity of transsubstantiation and transsignification, but it does free the question from merely physical considerations.

Passing to the consideration of the function of bread and wine in specifically religious symbolic activity, Schillebeeckx points out the fact that sacraments are not *things,* but human actions in which material objects function as conveyors of religious meaning and reality. In this context, he traces the function of bread and wine in the religious meal from a cosmic liturgical function through the Jewish religious paschal meal to the specifically Christian significance and power of the bread and wine in the Eucharistic action. In this context, too, the implied transsubstantiation which takes place is not simply directed toward the mere "presence of Christ"; the "visit with Jesus" is alien to the significance of the Eucharist. Its context is rather the participation in life which comes through Christ's death and resurrection.

Finally, in the context of this grace-meaning and grace-effect of the Eucharist, one can approach the peculiarity of Christ's real Eucharistic presence. The basis of all of this is Christ's gift of Himself to His fellow men and, through them, to the Father. The Eucharist is the sacramental visibility of this continuous self-giving. Bread and wine, in the context of the Eucharistic meal, lose thir profane significance and take on the meaning of this gift of self by Christ. The words of consecration are not simply directed toward the bread and wine; "This is my body . . . This is my blood" are words directed toward the believer. This real presence of Christ is directed toward them, but in and by means of this gift of bread and wine. Christ the Lord is, in other words, *sacramentally* present, present in an action of the gift of Himself. Thus bread and wine are given a new meaning, not by men, however, but by Christ the Lord acting in the Church. And this action of giving a new meaning to the bread and wine, since it takes place in the action of the Church, presupposes the presence of Christ in the Church, in the community gathered together in Eucharistic worship.

Schillebeeckx insists quite strongly that, in his opinion, Christ's presence in the Church is "co-constitutive" of the Eucharist itself. Scholasticism saw Christ's presence in the bread and wine and in heaven, considering His presence in the Church as simply the effect (the "fruit") of the Eucharist. But Schillebeeckx insists that if Christ's presence in the Church celebrating the Eucharist is left out of consideration, the very reality of His Eucharistic presence is deprived of much of its meaning and power. What is given in the Eucharist is not a *thing,* even if the thing in question is a glance of love from Christ; the gift is far deeper. Christ gives *Himself* to the Church in the gift of bread and wine. Thus, the bread and wine are signs in the maximal sense of the word: Christ literally gives *Himself* in this gift.

Further, the Eucharistic species do not simply signify and effect Christ's gift of Himself to the Church; they also signify and realize the Church's gift of itself to Christ. As a salvific community, the Church cannot be seen as something apart from Christ, and thus as Christ renders Himself present in the species, the Church renders itself present also. Together, Christ and His body, the Church, make themselves present and give themselves to the Father, to whom Eucharistic worship is directed. Christ's "Eucharistic body" is the communion of the Church with Christ, the realization of what is meant by the "body of the Lord." This is what is sacramentalized in the Eucharistic action.

All this means that, although the effect of the Eucharist and Christ's presence is not simply the effect of the faith of the individual, the mutuality of the meaning of the Eucharist means that it only reaches the fullness of its sacramental form in the mutual presence of Christ to His Church and of the individual in the Church of Christ and the Church in the act of communion (sacramental communion!) in the Eucharist. If the consecrated bread is viewed outside this context of Christ acting in the Church, it is rendered meaningless and beyond experience. Any physical or metaphysical analysis apart from this specifically sacramental context is useless for the understanding of the Eucharist.

Only against the background of this entire Eucharistic event, then, can one approach the question of transsubstantiation and transsignification. The question of whether they are identical or whether one implies the other is ultimately a question of reality itself as experienced in the Eucharist.

Reality is normally perceived in a complex act of the knower in which perception, understanding and all the complexity of the human act of the knowing subject come into play. Appearances normally are the "sign" of reality, containing the reality which they incarnate for the knowing subject. In the case of the Eucharist, however, the knowing subject is pulled up short. For what appears to be bread and wine is actually the "body of the Lord." Thus, there is a change in the signifying function of these appearances, but that change (a "transsignification") is a change precisely because the reality which is contained in these appearances is no longer the reality of bread and wine, but Christ's bodily reality. "Transsignification," in other words, presupposes "transsubstantiation." Though not simply identical, the two realities evoke one another and are inseparable. There is a metaphysical priority to the fact of transsubstantiation, but given that fact, it takes place in the context of a transsignification in which Christ manifests Himself to the believer in the community under the "sign" of bread and wine. Transsignification is brought about by the creative action of the Spirit of God in the action of the Eucharist.

If Schillebeeckx adds anything to the discussion (and he adds a great deal), it is primarily the soundness of his theological method which is the most significant factor of his participation in this discussion. His hermeneutical principles in the interpretation of the Council of Trent form a solid basis for his constructive reflection. He brings to mind the scribe who knows how to bring forth from his stores things both old and new (Mt 13:52).

September of 1965 saw the publication of "Mysterium Fidei" in *L'Osservatore Romano.* The amount of literature took another rise. Some of the literature attempted to present the positions of the new thought fairly;[29] some was critical, though perceptive;[30] some, especially some popularizing articles in the journals for priests, did not seem to understand the developments at all. A paper read at an ecumenical conference in England in 1962 by H. B. Greene was published in the *Downside Review,*[31] presenting the conflict of realism and symbolism in the theologies of the Eucharist. Appended to this paper was a résumé of a paper read by Charles Davis in Australia and subsequently published in *Sophia,* the journal of the school of philosophical theology at the University of Melbourne.

All of these presentations are interesting and merit serious consideration in their own right. However, a presentation of their content would amount to more repetition of ideas already perhaps too often repeated. They treat of what Trent did and did not impose on belief, presence, transsubstantiation, the reactions to the new developments, and so on. It would seem better to synthesize all the developments in a constructive reflection on the theological significance of the real presence of Christ in the Eucharist and the change which this demands in the Eucharistic Species.

### *The Mystery of the Eucharist*

Any consideration or presentation of the theology of the Eucharist must begin with the understanding that the Eucharist is a mystery. This implies several things. It implies, first of all, that the consideration and presentation cannot be considered explana-

29. J. M. Powers, S.J. '*Mysterium Fidei* and the Theology of the Eucharist," in *Worship* 40 (January, 1966), pp. 17–35; Schillebeeckx, "Transsubstantiation, Transfinalization, Transfiguration," in *Ibid.* (June), pp. 324–338.

30. J. Delmotte, "*Mysterium Fidei.* Recente publikaties over de Eucharistie," in *Coll. BG* 12 (1966), pp. 3–25 (Treats the writings of Schoonenberg, Sonnen, Smits, Schillebeeckx, Trooster); Coleman O'Niell, O.P., "What is 'transsignification' all about?", in *Catholic World* 202 (1965–66), pp. 204–210; G. Sloyan, "Real Presence: Debate on the Eucharist," in *Commonweal* 84 (1966), pp. 357–361.

31. Bibliography, n. 24.

tory in the sense that the human mind will end up with a full understanding of the reality of the Eucharist. On the contrary, it means that the theologian can only indicate more and more clearly the areas in which the mystery eludes the limitations of human knowledge. And this means that, although some appreciation of the Eucharist can be gained from the use of analogies based on one's own experience, these analogies pale in the face of the reality. Thus, the considerations which follow will draw on the analogies of "presence" and "change." But it must be kept in mind that even these consecrated expressions, associated for centuries with the teaching Church as they are, are still human language and do not break through to that which they convey only weakly. This, after all, is the basic failure in fundamentalism. It equates its own language with the reality of God and, logically enough, ends up in the worship of the constructions of its own language, a "logolatry." It should always be kept in mind, especially by the theologian, that relativism is not simply a sin of the liberal. A fundamentalist attitude, the attitude which insists that what one has been taught or has come to believe is the literal and unchanging truth about reality and especially about God, is as relativist as the attitude of one who refuses to commit himself to any truth on the ground that all truth is relative. The only way out of this Scylla and Charybdis is the constant correction of one's convictions by the fact that these are conveyed in analogies and do not by any means exhaust the reality. Thus, the reflection which follows does not pretend to "prove" or "solve" the Eucharist, because the Eucharist is not a thesis or a problem. It is a mystery; indeed, from man's point of view, it is *the* mystery, *mysterium fidei.*

*The Real Presence.* Contrary to Schelfhout's contention, the heart of the eucharistic mystery is not in the fact of transsubstantiation.[32] The core of this mystery is in the presence of Christ to the Church as the gift and root of its unity and worship. This is apparent even in the deliberations of the Council of Trent. In the sessions of 1551, the canon on transsubstantiation was on the

32. Cf. above, pp. 126–127.

verge of rejection because the council Fathers did not see that it added anything at all to the statement of the real presence. The council did not reason from transsubstantiation to the real presence, but just the opposite. In fact, it seems to have been Melchior Cano's opinion that one could accept the real presence without affirming transsubstantiation which eventually led to the incorporation of this canon.[33] This, together with Luther's contention that the very use of the word was a recent invention, led the council to defend the theological tradition of the Church in the framing of the second canon.

Further, to state that the real presence comes about by transsubstantiation is an unfortunate distortion of the context of transsubstantiation. It should be kept in mind that the Council of Trent was faced with very concrete problems and directed its action towards those problems. It did not make a total statement on the Eucharist, but only defended the faith of the Church in the real presence of Christ and the real change which the very reality of Christ's presence demands. Further, it should be kept in mind that Christ is really, truly, and objectively present in the Eucharist before the consecration. It is the action of Christ, not the action of man, which brings about transsubstantiation. The minister of the sacrament acts only in virtue of Christ's priestly power in the act of consecration. Unfortunately, since Scotus characterized the presence of Christ in the Eucharistic Species as "the" real presence, the context of transsubstantiation has been seen as that which "renders Christ present" when the opposite is true. It is precisely the presence and action of Christ in the Eucharist which effects transsubstantiation. Accordingly, before going into the question of transsubstantiation and "transsignification," one must carefully consider the basis and character of Christ's presence in the Eucharistic action.

The basis of the real presence of Christ in the Eucharist is found in the reality of the Eucharistic action itself. If this is a memorial of the Lord which merely recalls His past blessings,

33. *Concilium Tridentinum* (Ed. Görresgesellschaft), vol. 7 (Part IV, vol. 1, *Acta Concilii iterum Tridentinum congregati, a Massarello conscripta,* 1551–1552), pp. 125, 149–170 *et passim.*

there is no need for a "real presence." It is, in this view, simply the recollection of one who is simply not present, but whose actions in the dead past are the root of our faith in God and in Him. Again, if the Eucharist is simply an action in which the Church, as a human gathering, expresses her faith in herself as a community, the presence of Christ could be seen as a symbolic reality in the sense that in reality Christ is not present. A view of the Eucharist which sees it simply as a "symbolic memorial" views the Eucharist as a basically human action to which faith can attach a further meaning. But given the meaning which faith attaches, this could only be a pretense, acting "as if" Christ were present and no more. This however, is not the biblical faith in the Eucharist which the New Testament presents.

St. Paul presents the Eucharist in strongly realistic terms in his insistence on the reality of the union which is brought about in the Eucharistic action. This eating and drinking brings about the unity of the Church if it is truly celebrated as the "Lord's supper" (1 Cor 11:20). This action is communion in the sacrificial reality of Christ (11:14–18), it is the proclamation of the Lord's death in anticipation of His return (11:26). The failure of the Corinthians to discern this brings about the real judgment of God on their community (11:29–31). The action, in other words, is by no means a pretense, a mere recollection, but a true communion in the active saving reality of the Risen Jesus. To the extent that this real meaning and power is discerned in the action of the Eucharistic assembly, the unity of the Church, with all that this implies, is truly realized among the communicants. To the extent that it is not discerned, the judgment of God is levied against the life of the community as such.

The synoptic gospels stress the reality of the Eucharistic action in terms of the reality of the sacrifice of redemption which takes place in the death and resurrection of Jesus. Situating the Eucharistic action of Jesus against the background of the reality of the meaning and power of Passover, the synoptics see in His action the creative action in which Jesus gives the disciples the real meaning and real power of His coming death and resurrection. The reality of Passover lay in the celebration of the action in which God, in the creative gift of the covenant, constantly "graced" His people with the blessings of deliverance from bondage and their very existence as a unified people. It is unfortunate that the consideration of Passover as the foreshadowing of the Eucharist has pictured it as having no inner power. It is difficult to accept the contention that the Jewish ritual did not have a true sacramental meaning and power, that the faith of Israel in the power of her sacramental life was a delusion. Granted that Jesus transcendently fulfilled the promise which lay at the heart of the life and worship of Israel, granted that His sacrifice fulfilled every other sacrifice as the veil of the temple was torn in two, His action in the Last Supper was still a paschal action in which He, the Lord of the Sabbath, transformed the religious meaning and power of the Passover which His Father had given to His people. The "body" of the paschal sacrifice and meal is no longer the paschal lamb and unleavened bread; it is now given "for many" in the body of Jesus Himself. The covenant is no longer in the blood sprinkled at the altar of the temple; it is in the blood which Jesus shed for the remission of sins once and for all. It is in the reality of this redemption in the body and blood of Jesus that the realism of the Eucharistic action stands out in all its clarity.

St. John's Eucharistic realism is apparent from this meaning which he states is contained in the eating and drinking. This is eating the flesh of the Son of man and drinking His blood (6:51, 53–58). And the meaning which is really contained in this eating and drinking is that eternal life which, when a man possesses it, will never let him die. This is the life which has been in the Word from the beginning (1:4). It is the life of God given to men in Jesus, so that the man who eats and drinks His flesh and blood abides in Him and shares His life. This eating and drinking is "spirit and life," no matter how scandalous it may seem to human reason (6:63). Expressed in John's own language, this gives the same basic religious reality to the Eucharist as do the presentations of the synoptic gospels and Paul. The "life" which is realized in the Eucharist is the life of the Church and of the believer in the Church, it is the life of redemption from sin by the death and resurrection of Jesus. John presents the Eucharistic action in its reality as a life-giving action. Without it, man cannot have that life which is "in Him."

The Letter to the Hebrews, though it does not develop the theology of the Eucharist explicitly, speaks in strongly realistic terms of the action of worship which is the Church's worship in Christ. It points out that the Church's worship, "our entry to the sanctuary," is in Christ's blood (10:19). Just as He entered the sanctuary of God's Holy of Holies once and for all in the accomplishment of a perfect sacrifice (7:27; 9:11–14, 24), we now have access to God's mercy through Him. The glorified Christ, then, is man's constant intercessor in a timeless act of priestly worship before God (4:14; 7:25; 8:1–2). In this way, God has given to man a timelessly effective action of worship in the gift of a perfect priest, a perfect offering, a perfect sacrifice (7:15–28). The Eucharistic worship of the Church, then, is a real action of worship, and this not in any human sense. It is God's gift of authentic worship in the gift of Christ.

It is on this basis, then, that the real presence can be seen: the basis of the reality of the action which is performed in the Eucharist, the reality of the gift of the unity of the Church in the flesh and blood of Christ, the reality of the redemptive power of the Eucharist in the same Christ, the reality of the life which is communicated in His flesh and blood, the reality of God's gift of authentic worship in Christ. It cannot be stressed too strongly that this action is real. It must be stressed that this action is real because it is Christ's action first and foremost, not man's action. Man cannot offer perfect sacrifice to God of Himself, He cannot gather Himself into a unity as God's people, He cannot grasp the life of God, or the gift of redemption by some Promethean struggle. Only God can give these gifts to man. And God has given these gifts in Christ.

On this basis, then, some appreciation of the character of Christ's presence in the Eucharist can be approached. The reality of His presence, as we have seen, is seen in the reality of the action which He performs in and through the action of the Church at worship in Him and with Him. Human paradigms are useful for some appreciation of the mystery of the Eucharist, and

Schoonenberg's studies in the reality of "presence" are useful in their presentation of the reality of personal presence.[34] What emerges from that presentation is the fact that although real presence must have an objective basis, the objective basis itself does not realize presence on the level on which it takes place. Thus, the mere spatial relationship of even the objects of nature is not the principle of their local presence to one another. Action is of the essence of presence. This is, of course, all the more true on the level of personal presence. The objective juxtaposition of a number of persons in a defined location is the basis for the reality of personal presence and relationship coming into operation, but it does not constitute personal presence. The reason for this is that personal presence only comes into operation in the confrontation of subjectivities. Only when one sees another person as the source of truly personal activity directed toward one's self can personal presence come into operation. And the fullness of that presence can only be said to be real to the extent that a genuine encounter of two personal realities takes place in the mutual confrontation of the personal "interior" of each person. Thus, personal presence is necessarily mediated by bodily presence, but it is more than that. This is very important for the understanding of the language which contemporary theologians are using in their treatment of the Eucharistic presence of Jesus. It can be seen that genuine personal presence is basically a "spiritual" reality; it consists in the confrontation of free consciousnesses. Thus, the statement that Christ's presence is "spiritual" by no means indicates that He is not truly and objectively present in the fullness of His personal reality. On the contrary, it stresses the fact that one cannot properly speak of Christ's presence in simple physical terms and hope to convey the religious reality. Further, the statement that Christ's presence is "symbolic" by no means implies that it is not real. This means, rather, that there is a reality in the action of the Eucharist which is basically the reality of Christ's gift of Himself to the Church and everyone in the Church in the sacramental reality of the Eucharist. The Eucharist is primarily Christ's action in which He associates the Church with Himself in His worship of the Father, but in this

34. Cf. above, pp. 121–125, 134–139.

action He gives Himself really, truly and objectively to the Church in and by means of the sign-act in which He reveals Himself to the Church. Sign is not opposed to reality. It is rather the incarnation of reality.

Before going into the sacramental character of Christ's presence, however, it is important to draw a distinction between the objectivity of His presence and the "objectifiability" of Christ.[35] The objectivity of His presence stresses the fact of the "givenness" of His presence. It means that His presence is not simply the construction of man's faith. Christ's presence precedes man's faith, though it is not unrelated to faith. His presence is in the act in which He gives Himself and all His salvific reality to man in continuous need of redemption. It is a presence, then, which is aimed at subjectivity, the appropriation in faith of the gift of Christ. This objective character of Christ's presence, however, does not mean that Christ is "objectifiable" in the Eucharist, or at any other time or place. For the Christ who is present is the glorified Lord, no longer existing in the conditions of earthly existence.

It is precisely at this point that the human paradigms of personal presence break down. Granted that these are useful for an analogous understanding of the fact that Christ's presence is not simply a material fact, but that His presence demands a religious response from the believer for its full interpersonal reality, the fact that the Risen Christ is not an objectifiable reality brings out the transcendent difference between His condition and the earthly human condition, bound as it is to the limitations of a spatio-temporal existence. In the human condition, real objective personal presence only comes about as the foundation for genuine personal relationships to the extent that the bodily reality of one personal subject confronts that of another. Men are, after all, bound to the conditions of living in time and space. Human knowledge is essentially bound to the sensible perception of another as "object" before the reality of an intersubjectivity can come about. It has been seen that intersubjectivity transcends this "objectivity" and outlasts it, but it is the basic condition of personal presence of any kind. The exact opposite is true of the

35. Cf. above, pp. 104–108.

Risen Jesus, however. He does not live subject to time and space. It is the sovereign freedom of His gift of Himself which makes Him objectively present in the manifestations which occur after the resurrection. There is no "objective" presence which precedes this free gift of Himself. Jesus does not first make Himself present and then give Himself to the faith and devotion of His disciples; rather, His gift of Himself is His presence. There are certain foreshadowings of this fully "personalized" bodily reality of Jesus in the walking on the water (Mt 14:25–33) and in the Transfiguration (Mt 17:1–8). In both cases, what happens is the same, a fully "personalized" bodily manifestation of the Son of God in His bodily reality, freed from the pedestrian human condition, a manifestation which reveals in a bodily fashion the glory of the Son of God, a manifestation which evokes the adoration of the disciples. It is the free gift of this manifestation of Himself in His full personal reality which renders Him present in a bodily presence which breaks through the spatio-temporal limitations of human existence and shows the divine—in a bodily form. Jesus is truly man, it is true, but His human reality is not the reality of any man whomsoever. His humanity is the perfect organ of His personal reality, subject completely to His personal and sovereign freedom.

Christ is really, truly and objectively present in the Eucharist, then, but this reality, truth and objectivity must not be seen in a physicistically univocal view of His presence as corresponding to human modes of presence in this earthly condition. His presence is not subject to the control of human knowledge. He cannot be "noted"; He is not "there to be seen" previous to His gift of Himself. But this does not mean that He is not really present. He is present and His presence is that of the Risen Jesus, sovereignly free of human limitations in the gift of Himself. Once again, it can be seen that the reality of His presence corresponds to the reality of the action of the Eucharist. If the gift is real, true, objective, His presence is real, true, objective. Perhaps these thoughts will make no sense to the mind which identifies objectivity with objectifiability. One can only insist in reply on the essential necessity of an analogous understanding of the reality of the Risen Jesus. Analogy, after all, is unity in basic distinction, similarity in basic dissimilarity. Granted, then, that Christ's presence in the Eucharist is real, true and objective, this presence, though like human personal presence, is deeply different because of the deep difference between the bodily condition of the Risen Jesus and the human bodily condition at the present time.

There is another aspect of the bodily reality of the Risen Jesus which also breaks down the human paradigms of personal presence and their too literal application to the theology of the Eucharist. This is the fact that the body of the Lord, that "bit of the world in which He lives personally," is not simply the individuality of His human reality but is, in the real bond of the Spirit, the whole of the Church. It is essential to note, of course, that this fact does not eliminate the human individuality of Jesus; it does not mean, in Schoonenberg's words, that Jesus coincides personally with the Church or that His personal reality is absorbed by the Church.[36] What it does mean is that Jesus personally subsists not only in His own human individuality, but also in a union with His Church which, in the personal reality, action, and function of the one Spirit in Jesus and in the Church, transcends even the unity of body and spirit in man. This is important for the theology of the Eucharist, because if, as St. Thomas has stated and Pope Paul has reiterated in "Mysterium Fidei," the Eucharist is the sign and cause of the unity of the Church, it is because the body of Christ is to be understood in terms broader than those of the human individuality which is known to this earthly existence. It is true that the concern of the Council of Trent centered mainly on the objectivity of the presence of Christ in the Eucharist, on the fact that His presence is not the construction or the effect of man's faith. Thus, it stressed Christ's presence as true (as opposed to merely symbolic), real (as opposed to a figurative interpretation of the accounts of institution) and substantial (as opposed to the presence of the "power of Christ" alone). Thus, the emphasis on the *"totus Christus"* (the whole Christ) whose presence is affirmed with such strength in the first chapter of the Decree on the Holy Eucharist, is an emphasis on the true personal presence of the

36. Cf. above, pp. 107–108.

Christ whose body, blood, soul and divinity are one in the indissoluble unity of the hypostatic unity of the incarnate Son of God. Vatican II, however, has enlarged the perspective in which this presence can be stated. The "whole Christ" is stated in terms of the unity of Christ and His Church in the Eucharist, present in His members who form the elements of the celebrating community. In the dogmatic constitution on the Church, the Council comes to speak of the presence of the Church in Christ in its statement that the whole life of the Church is offered to the Father together with the offering of the body of the Lord.[37] Here is a return to the language of Paul and Augustine, to the effect that the Christians are the body of Christ, that the reception of the body of the Lord is the reception of what the Christian community is, Christ's body. Perhaps now one can return to the statement of Alger of Liège that the whole Church is "con-corporal and co-sacramental with Christ on the altar"[38] without having to fear that this will be seen as some type of christological

37. Sacrosanctum Oecumenicum Concilium Vaticanum Secundum, *Constitutio Dogmatica de Ecclesia,* n. 34 (Ed. Vatican City: Polyglot Press, 1964, p. 40). "All their [the laity's] works, their prayers and apostolic endeavors, their conjugal and family life, their daily work, their relaxation of mind and body, if these are performed in the Spirit, indeed the troubles of life, if they are patiently borne, —all these become spiritual offerings acceptable to God through Jesus Christ (1 Pet 2:5), which are offered to God with deepest piety in the celebration of the Eucharist, together with the offering of the body of the Lord."

38. *De Sacramento Corporis et Sanguinis Dominici,* Lib. III, c. 12 (*PL* 180, col. 847). "When it is said that it is not the body of the Lord which the schismatic consecrates because the Eucharist cannot be consecrated among people like this, this is not to be understood in the sense that the essentially true body of Christ is not consecrated in the sacrament; rather, it is to be understood in the sense that, since the Church is con-corporal and co-sacramental with Christ on the altar, he does not consecrate the whole body of Christ, viz., the Head together with the members, —who, since he is outside the Church, does not unite himself to Christ and the Church in what is the sacrament of both. For since the sacrifice of the altar, signifying the unity of the Church herself with Christ, is the sacrament of the whole body of Christ, it is not brought about where the whole Christ is not confected." (For a discussion of the questions of the power to consecrate among schismatics in the early middle ages and the classical question of what the mouse eats when it eats a consecrated host, cf. A. M. Landgraf, "Zur Lehre von der Konsekrationsgewalt des von der Kirche getrennten Priesters" and "Die in der Frühscholastik klassische Frage *quid sumit mus,*" in *Dogmengeschichte der Frühscholastik,* Bd. III: *Die Lehre von den Sakramenten,* pp. 223–243, 207–222.)

pantheism. As Vatican II has brought out, this is a presence of Christ in His Church and the Church in Him which is ultimately the presence of the whole Christ to His Father and ours in the perfectly authentic act of worship.

Finally, it must be seen what is involved in the fact that this real presence is a sacramental presence. A sacramental presence is a presence in a symbolic act. Our age is cynical about symbolic acts precisely because of their frequent lack of real content. Thus, it is essential to recall what has been said thus far about the reality of this action of the Eucharist. The reality of the presence of Christ is based precisely on the fact that this really is the action of Christ and that it really brings about what is "signified." It is a real sacrifice, a really authentic gift of worship in Christ, ultimate real principle of the unity of the Church, the real memorial-celebration of the death of the Lord, the real prefiguring of the life of the world to come. Christ is objectively present to the Church and in the Church to the Father. The "whole Christ" is present in this act which is God's own gift of worship. But, at the same time, and in all the reality of this presence, Christ is still sacramentally present, present in a sign-act.

The mention of the word "sign," of course, immediately causes problems in many minds. Under the influence (conscious or unconscious) of the post-Kantian dualism, many restrict the consideration of the reality of the sign to the gnoseological sphere, seeing the sign as an already constituted physical reality to which the mind assigns an alien or abstract "significance": when one thing is seen, something else is understood. Consequently, the stress which contemporary theology is placing on the reality of the sign in the theology of the sacraments always raises the question "What is meant here by 'sign'?"[39]

The anthropological appreciation of the reality of the sign-act has been presented already.[40] What is important to note in this appreciation of the sign is the fact that it is not simply a "thing." The sign-act is an action, and the reality of the sign can only be

39. This is the question which underlies the criticisms which Delmotte, for example, addresses to a number of the contemporary expositions of transsignification (Bibliography, n. 31).

40. Cf. above, pp. 81–86.

understood in terms of the totality of the sign-act. At the heart of the sign-act is the personal reality which is expressed and given in the expression; the sign-act is basically an act of self-communication, of self-participation to other persons. This is what is ultimately "signified," it is the basic "significance" of the sign-act. This self-communication, as has also been seen, takes place primarily in the unique organ of self-communication, the bodily dimension of human life. The totality of the sign-act, then, consists in the incarnation of personal intention in bodily gesture, communicating with other bodily constituted persons. But man also takes up the material world which surrounds him into this action of self-expression and -communication, and in this action, the material world becomes the instrument of self-communication.

On the human level, one can proceed to ask the question of the physical reality of these instruments. An example will help here. A boy gives a ring to a girl. The setting of this gift is a marriage ceremony or an engagement. One can consider the physical reality of the ring. It is of gold, it has a diamond set into it. If it is considered apart from the action in which it is given, it is simply so much metal and so much carbon which has been compressed into this form by a number of geological influences. But such a consideration leaves out a great deal of the reality—yes, the reality—of the ring. What has been given is not simply so much gold and so much carbon. The diamond has been chosen with a great deal of care; the gold has been shaped and chosen for a very particular finger. All of this has gone into the very physical shape of the metal and carbon. It has been shaped, physically shaped, in other words, in order to have the capacity to express a personal intention: the constancy of a man's love for a woman. But this is not all. The man himself has placed it on her finger, in a very real "physical" context. Words, actions and this instrument have been taken up into the physical unity of an action which incarnates the personal intention of the constant love of a man for a woman. Once again, one can look at the physical realities involved; one can parse the words used, one can analyze the physical reality of the muscular movements involved in speaking and the placing of the ring. What is the result? Nothing. For this type of analysis has ignored the only reality which is the moving force behind all these physical realities. It has not seen what has brought it all to pass: the love of man and woman. One might say that this is true, but that these are extrinsic to the physical realities involved. But this can only be said by one who completely ignores the very real physical components of a very real moment in the history of two lives, a physical reality which really calls these two to become "one flesh." The concomitance of all these physical realities has only one basis, their real unity in the sign-act in which a man really expresses the constancy of his love for a woman. If this is not real, nothing is. The "physical" reality of the historical moment is more, far more than the "physical" realities of muscles, sounds, metals involved. Words, gestures and instrument are all one only in the fact that they contain, in this very real moment, an effective meaning communicated from one person to another. It is that meaning which dominates the "physical" realities involved in a real action. It is not simply a question of man's assigning an abstract meaning to material elements; it is a question of the real incarnation of meaning in these elements. When the woman later drops the ring down the garbage-disposal unit, she doesn't look at it as so much metal. She takes the unit apart precisely because the ring is so very much more, really more.

One might ask what kind of mind it is which concentrates on physical realities and says that the ring is gold or it is not. That type of mind would say that it is "objective." It views things as they are. But one wonders whether it would not be better described as "objectifying," considering everything in its objective state and ignoring the genuine personal realities involved in the historical moment. One can, after all, even objectify love, reduce it to the status of a "thing," consider, analyze, poke at it. But this objectified love is an abstraction, not a reality. It is only in loving that love is existentially real. Love can be measured, of course, in so many ways, biologically, chemically, psychologically, but these are only analyses of the physical manifestations of something which is real but not physical in its essence.

But all of this is stated by way of analogy. It is useful to illustrate the reality of the sign-act and what is involved in the fullness of its reality. After all, the capacity which man has to assign meaning to the material world in which He lives is limited by the objective capacity of that world to convey his intentions. Man cannot mix water, yeast and arsenic and assign the meaning of nourishment to it, for the simple reason that arsenic does not nourish, it kills. And this is all the more true on the level of God's relationship with man. For on that level the creative initiative belongs absolutely to God. Man's role there is not creative or determinative; it is one of openness to the creative fidelity of God's unfailing love for man. In this order, man is more creature than in any other, because the creative initiative belongs absolutely to God, man can only receive, he cannot give. For what is involved in the order of grace is the sovereignly free communication of God's own life to man. Man has absolutely no capacity to reach up and grasp that life. And this is true in the sacramental life of the Church no less than elsewhere. The gift of the sacraments is always God's creative gift to man. The ritual does not charm grace out of heaven. It is God's absolutely free gift of God. It is the gift of His presence and power saving, sanctifying, redeeming man.

The Eucharistic presence of Christ is, then, a sacramental presence. Basically, this means that it is His presence in a sign-act. But this sign-act is not man's act. It is God's. This cannot be emphasized too strongly. It is the action in which Christ gives Himself to man in and by means of the cultic action of the Church. In the bond of the Spirit, Christ acts through the prayer and profession of the Church to give Himself to man as his saviour. This is Christ's action, an action in which He associates the Church with Himself in the Spirit (and this is real, not simply "spiritual") as his instrument. The reality of the role of the Spirit in this action cannot be overlooked, as it so often has. It is precisely in the Spirit that the Church's ministers can act in the name and person of Christ. If the character means anything at all, it basically means an incorporation into Christ's priestly reality so that Christ's action of worship is active in the Church in the community of the baptized and ordained. And the reality of God's gift of His own life to man is basically the reality of the constant gift of the Spirit, the Gift in whom every gift is given. For the personal reality and the personal function of the Spirit is precisely that of being the bond between persons. In the Trinity, the Spirit is the ineffable personal bond between Father and Son. In the dispensation of salvation, the one Spirit, in Christ and in the Christian, is the bond in whom Christ and His body are one. It is thus that the action of the Church is really the action of Christ, giving Himself to the world in the visibility of the action of the Church. The Church is the sacrament of Christ, as Christ is the sacrament of God. Her action is sacramental only because of her unity with this primal sacrament, the visible gift of God to man, the "giving manifestation" of grace. The sacrament is not a thing, in other words; the sacrament is an action of God performed in the visibility of the Church.

Against this background, then, it can be seen that the Eucharistic presence of Christ is a presence in a sign. But the sign of that presence is not simply the physical reality of bread. The sign in which Christ is present is the worshipping community, the people at prayer, the celebrant proclaiming the words of consecration, and the bread and wine in this context of sacramental action. It is Christ who prays in the Church, it is Christ who proclaims the words of consecration, it is Christ whose word renders Him present in the Eucharistic Species as the sign of His intimate and complete union with the communicant. This is not an action in which man assigns a meaning to the celebrating congregation. Rather, it is an action in which Christ expresses Himself, gives Himself to the community and to the individual in the community through the action of the Church which He associates with Himself. This is not a meaning which is superimposed on the worshipping community by man's mind, or even by Christ's mind. It is rather the very inner reality of the action itself. The symbol, the sign-act is not opposed to reality, it is rather the very incarnation of the deepest reality. It is in this context that one can begin to understand what is involved in the use of the expressions "transsignification" and "transfinalization."

*Transsignification and transsubstantiation.* It is sometimes proposed that the idea of transsignification is presented as an alternative to the traditional theological idea of transsubstantiation.[41] Doubtless this is true in some cases. It has been remarked in the press, at least, that some theologians feel that this expression brings the theology of the Eucharist into the 20th century. Theologians of a more traditional cast of thought have reacted against what might well seem to be an excessively existentialistic point of departure: the existentialist primitive insight that human existence is the prime paradigm of existence and that everything else only has meaning only in terms of man. The relativism of this position is apparent and it would pose a serious threat not only to the theology of the Eucharist, but to the whole of theology, not to mention the very foundation of religion itself: the openness of man to a reality which transcends his own condition. However, it should be pointed out that the atheistic existentialism of Sartre and the agnostic phenomenology of Merleau-Ponty are not the only existentialist world-views. The existentialism of Marcel and the later phenomenology of Heidegger are open to transcendence and bring to the theologian the possibility of the elaboration of a theology which gives far more place to the realities of history and human intentionality. And, granted the agnosticism or postulatory atheism of some existentialists, this does not mean that the whole of their world-view is thereby invalid. Atheism is not, after all, a logical necessity for this world-view; it is rather a postulated necessity for some existentialists. Thus it is that a Christian existentialism is not only possible, but is positively fruitful, as is apparent from the theologies of Rahner, Schillebeeckx, Schoonenberg and others. To a solid grasp of the tradition of the Church these men have added a fresh and vibrant contemporary view of man and his world which has given a fruitful orientation to theology in

41. Cf. Coleman O'Neill, O.P., "What is transsignification all about?", in *Catholic World* 202 (1965–1966), pp. 204–210; O. Schelfhout (Bibliography, n. 16); J. Delmotte (Bibliography, n. 31). Leenhardt, followed by de Baciocchi and others, speaks in terms of a "transfinalization," while Smits and Schoonenberg speak in terms of "transsignification." The terms are reductively identical and "transsignification" will be used for both.

the treatment of the great mysteries of the Trinity, Incarnation, Church, sacraments and grace. It is in the light of the contributions of these men that the treatment of transsignification makes religious and theological sense.

It has been indicated already that the fundamental theological location of the idea of transsignification is not simply in the theology of the Eucharist, but in the question of the institution of all the sacraments.[42] Transsignification basically means the divine (not human!) act in which the substance (that is, the meaning and power) of a religious sign is transformed in the personal revelation of God. It has been seen that transsignification takes place on the level of the ritual religion of Israel because the whole life of Israel is interiorly transformed in the personal revelation of Yahweh as Israel's God. In this, the very reality of Israel as a people becomes a religious sign to the world of the presence and power of Yahweh. Thus, even though the outward shape of Israel's religious ritual may not differ from that of other nomadic or semi-nomadic tribes of the Near East, the inner meaning and power of her ritual is radically transformed in the presence and power of Yahweh at the heart of her life as a people. It has also been seen how the coming of Christ interiorly transforms the ritual religion of Israel in the transformation of the very life of Israel. St. Paul's contrast between the "Israel of the flesh" (1 Cor 10:18, Rom 7:5) and the "Israel of God" (Gal 6:16) brings out the continuity-in-discontinuity between Israel and the Christian community. Basically, this transsignification of the religious sign (the sacrament) of Israel takes place in the messianic reality of Jesus Himself.[43] In the life of the apostolic Church, then, even though there may be relatively little difference between this community and the community of Israel, its whole life has a transformed inner meaning and power: the reality of the Risen Jesus, the Lord. Thus, though the primitive Church may continue much of the religious ritual of Israel (Baptism, cultic repentance, laying on of hands in ordination and

42. Cf. above, pp. 48–58.

43. Cf. Schillebeeckx, *Christ the Sacrament of the Encounter with God,* pp. 10–13.

in confirmation as the sign of the gift of the Spirit of God, anointing of the sick, etc.), the inner meaning and power of this ritual is the fulfillment of all the promise which lay at the heart of Israel's life as a people and of her ritual religion. The religious ritual of the Christian community is the celebration of the salvific reality of the Risen Jesus, the gift of redemption and worship from His Father.

The reality of the transsignifying action of Christ in the Eucharist has already been presented.[44] We have seen how, in the context of the memorial-celebration of Passover, Jesus gave new meaning to the sacramental reality of the paschal meal. His own body becomes the "body" of the paschal celebration, replacing the reality of the lamb and the unleavened bread. The reason for this is that a new deliverance is given by God in the body of Christ in the crucifixion and resurrection. His command "Do this for my remembrance" is the gift of the continual celebration of this deliverance until it is ultimately fulfilled in the day when God's promise will be completely fulfilled and He will be "all in all." In the very celebration of the paschal meal, then, without altering the physical shape of the celebration, Jesus did change the interior reality of the celebration in his changing of the inner meaning and power of the celebration. He is the paschal lamb, the "lamb of God," given by God for the salvation of the world; the new covenant is a covenant given in His blood, shed for the remission of sins, the great eschatological judgment of God against sin and its power in the world.

Another point is important here. Unfortunately, the question of the reality of the Eucharist has come to center too exclusively on the reality of the "substance of bread" and the "substance of Christ's body." But even critics of the idea of transsignification will admit that the "substance of bread" or the "substance of His body" were not what was in Jesus' mind in His action in the Last Supper.[45] What was in His mind was the fact that, in His death and resurrection, the central meaning and power which God had given to the celebration of Passover was to be transcendently

44. Cf. above, pp. 53–64.
45. O'Neill, *art. cit.*, p. 209.

fulfilled in His body. It is in Jesus that God will gather together a new people, deliver men from the bondage of sin, grant a new gift of perfect worship. Thus, His words "This is my body, given for you . . . This is my blood, shed for many" must be seen in the context of the paschal celebration and the religious meaning and power of the unleavened bread and the cup of benediction. In other words, it is not a question of the substantial reality of bread and wine as existing material objects. It is rather a question of the substance of bread and wine on a different level, the level of their symbolic reality and their effective symbolic power. Only against the sacramental realism of the celebration of Passover does the real content of the action of Jesus become clear in its fullness. His action is the true gift of Himself as the body of the New Pasch.

The reality of this action, of course, means that Jesus really does give Himself, that what He gives to His disciples really is Himself, body, blood, soul, divinity, all. Transsignification does not preclude a real conversion of the substantial reality of the unleavened bread and the cup of benediction into the substantial reality of Jesus. Rather, it demands that true conversion. The reality of the action of Jesus demands the reality of His sacramental presence and the reality of the conversion. If the memorial which He commands is to be real, if the sacrifice offered to God is to be real, if the unity of the new people is to be real, He must really give Himself, not just a symbol of Himself in the abstract sense of the word. It cannot be stressed too strongly: the reality of Christ's transsignifying action demands the reality of His presence and of the true conversion. But to see the action of Jesus as simply taking some bread and changing it into His body is to deprive His action of its central reality: its meaning. And the meaning of His action can only be seen when it is set into the context of His transsignification of what is essentially a sign-act, a symbolic celebration, a sacramental reality in Israel. With Schoonenberg, one must remark that transsubstantiation takes place in a transsignification, a transfinalization.[46]

46. *Art. cit.* (Bibliography, n. 22), p. 415.

The reality of the action of transsignification should be apparent on the level of the institution of the Eucharist, but this, of itself, does not respond to the question of the action of the Eucharist as it is celebrated at the present. To be sure, the Eucharist is celebrated daily in the Church now in fulfillment of the command of Jesus to do this in His remembrance. It is a command to do what He did on the night before He died. It is the same action which He enjoins: eating of this bread and drinking of this cup. Does this mean that the Eucharist today is a transsignification of the paschal sacrifice and the paschal meal as sacramental participation in that sacrifice? The answer to this question must be both negative and affirmative. On the negative side, it must be said that the context of the celebration of the Eucharist today is not that of the paschal meal. Gone are the bitter herbs, the haggadah, the paschal lamb, the temple sacrifice. In their place is the liturgy of the Word, proclaiming the new covenant, the New Law, the New Way in Christ. Not every celebration of the Eucharist contains the transition from the old covenant to the new as did the Last Supper. This is precisely the historical uniqueness of that event, and to think that one can evoke it somehow again would be a form of historical Docetism which robs the historical event of its initerable character. That moment can never occur again.

On the other hand, it should be noted that the Eucharist is, was, and will be the action of Christ, associating the Church with Himself in His timeless worship of the Father. This is the action of Jesus who could say to the Jews, "Before Abraham came to be, I am" (Jn 8:58). Thus, though the action of Jesus at the Last Supper was genuinely historical, and participated in the irreversible character of human history, it must also be maintained that the personal root of that action is the timeless actuality of the Son of God. In other words, the sacrificial reality of Jesus Christ is the same "yesterday, today, and forever" (Heb 13:8). Now as then, His action is the gift of worship in the transsignification of the human ritual action in which the community offers itself to God as it offers "spiritual sacrifices to God through Jesus Christ" (1 Pet 2:5). In the unleavened bread and the cup of benediction there is a certain historical continuity with the faith of Israel, but the bond between the Eucharist and the Last Supper is more than that of a religious-cultural rooting. The real bond is in the fact that Jesus performs the same action now which He did then, interiorly transforming the worship of a community and the community itself in its worship. It is only in the context of this action that one can speak meaningfully of change, of conversion.

In this context, then, it can be seen that the Christian community does not offer God a wafer of bread and a cup of wine and pray that it be changed into the body and blood of Christ. A colleague has remarked that it takes a greater act of faith to believe that what is present on the altar before the consecration is bread than to believe that it is Christ after the consecration. This is probably true, but it misses the point somewhat. What is on the altar and what is offered to God is not simply the physical reality of bread, or the "substance of bread." What is offered to God is the life of the community, already symbolized in the bread. And this life, like this bread, is offered to be changed. It is unfortunate that the discussion of transsignification and transsubstantiation so often centers on the question of physical substance and fails to see that the entire context of the reality of the bread is that of a sign-act. Such a myopic concentration on the substance of bread and the substance of the body of Christ ends up with a cosmological miracle devoid of any significant religious setting.

Further, it must be stressed most emphatically that the symbolic power of the bread and cup as elements in the sign-act of the celebrating community is not based on the human act of assigning this meaning to the bread and cup. The symbolic power is rooted in the words of Christ, "Do this for my remembrance." It is not simply an abstract relation of bread to a human intention. The symbolic power of the bread and cup is very real, rooted in the history of salvation and the offering of unleavened bread to God, man's creator and the creator of every gift for man. As Israel offered this bread to God and ate of it, the very life of the people was renewed in the on-going gift of the covenant-relation with God. As the Church offers this bread to God, she offers her own life, looking to the renewed gift of that life in the transformation of the bread into the gift of Christ. Further, this offering itself is not simply a human act. The offering is taken up by Christ into His own timeless actuality, into His continuous oblation of Himself to the Father.

What takes place in the consecration, then, is not simply the change of bread into body, wine into blood. What takes place basically is Christ's gift of Himself to the Church. He gives Himself, the whole of His timeless sacrificial reality before the Father, to the worshipping community as its offering, its sacrifice, its life. It is His word, not man's, which changes the bread and the cup into the signs of His giving. And the reality of the sign lies in the fact that in the totality of the action Christ is giving Himself, sharing Himself with the community through the bond of His Spirit.

In the totality of this sign-act, the act in which Christ gives Himself, one can situate the physical reality of the bread and wine. The symbolic capacity which they possess from Christ's command is transformed in the act of consecration, transformed by Christ's word from the sign which truly contains the offering of the Church into the sign which truly contains Christ's gift of Himself. It is in the genuine reality of this transsignification, in the change of the meaning of this bread and wine in the concrete action of the Eucharist, that the substantial realities involved are changed. Transsubstantiation takes place in transsignification. A man places the apparent physical reality of bread on another man's tongue; this is seen, heard, felt. But the reality which takes place in all of this is that Christ gives Himself to the communicants, to the Church. In this action, the cultic power which is at the heart of the reality of what is called the "character" of baptism and ordination, is actualized by the fact that Christ Himself, through the bond of the Spirit, associates the community with Himself, acting through it to offer its worship to His Father. What is important to see in all of this is that one cannot speak of bread and wine as signs unless one situates them in a concrete sign action. Bread and wine are not signs of Christ apart from this action; they do not have this symbolic capacity apart from His command, "Do this for my remembrance." Only in the context of the sign-act can one speak of the reality of what is used as a sign.

Given this context, then, one can speak of the conversion which takes place in the consecration, the true conversion which is true precisely because the sign action is true in its totality. It contains the grace reality which Christ expresses through it; or, in more traditional terms, it contains the grace it "signifies." The Eucharist contains the gift of Christ, *the* grace-gift, given to man in the physical reality of bread and wine. The reality is Christ's gift, not the action of man or the merely physical reality of bread and wine. And this reality is only available to man in another gift of Christ—faith. One cannot find the reality which underlies the sacrament by "unmasking" the celebrant or the community and seeing Christ or by analyzing the bread or wine with an electronic microscope. This change is not a change in molecular structure. Christ is not "under" or "behind" or "inside" the physical realities involved in the action of the Eucharist. But He does give Himself in the complexity of the physical realities involved. He gives Himself in His own way, in sovereign freedom, from all the conditions of our material existence. He gives Himself, in short, in mystery. Man cannot "note" or objectify Him, man can only receive His gift of Himself.

One final remark. J. Delmotte, in his criticisms of Schoonenberg's work, speaks of the "silence" in which Christ communicates Himself to those who receive Him, and stresses the fact that the presence and action of Christ in the Church and her Eucharist is "spiritual." He expresses concern that this "spirituality" of Christ's presence and the "silence" of His action be lost in the presentation of the reality of presence in a sign as Schoonenberg presents it. This concern reflects Delmotte's deeper question, a question which he places to almost all of the authors whose writings he presents. That question is the question of the sacramental sign itself. He seems to see the sacramental action as an action of the Church which somehow "veils" what is really taking place, so that the Church does one thing while Christ does something else. The Church sings, prays, while Christ communicates Himself to the members of the community "in silence," "The Lord is silent." In this view of the sacrament, the reality of the sign is seen as an objectively constituted complex of human actions which has a somewhat abstract relation to a "meaning" extrinsically assigned by Christ. What this kind of sacramental dualism misses is the fact that the action of Christ is incarnate precisely in the action of the celebrating community. This is the deepest reality of the instrumental function of the sacraments. These are sign-acts, acts in which Christ expresses His own salvific reality to the community in the community's celebration of Him, and acts in which He gives Himself to the community precisely in and by means of the communal action of the Church. Of course, in all of this it is absolutely essential to see the real personal function of the Spirit at work, one and the same Spirit in Christ and the community, constituting by His binding function that "one mystical person" who is the fullness of Christ. Only in this very realistic view of the body of Christ can the true instrumentality of the sacraments be fully appreciated. It is only in that one Spirit that the community can pray and offer itself to God "through Christ, our Lord." It is only in that same Spirit that Christ can speak through His minister to the community, "This is my body, given for you . . . This is my blood shed for many." Only in the one Spirit in Christ and in the community can the memorial, the sacrifice, the gift be real. And only in the reality of this memorial, sacrifice and gift can the real presence of Christ and the truth of the conversion of the physical realities involved be appreciated in the fullness of its religious meaning and realism.

With this realistic understanding of the body of Christ and its fullness, one can come to see, hear, feel Christ present in the community. One can come to see that the support which the voices of many lend to the voice of each individual is not simply a social human phenomenon, but is the comfort, the strength, the peace of Christ Himself shared in very human terms through those who are bound to Him in His Spirit. It is this visibility of

Christ in His gift which is the aim of renewal in the liturgy and theology of the Eucharist. To the extent that it enriches the life of the Church in and beyond the Eucharistic celebration, it is successful.

# APPENDIX TO CHAPTER FOUR

## *Selected Bibliography of Current Eucharistic Studies*

(ARRANGED CHRONOLOGICALLY)


*1955*

1. Leenhardt, Franz J., *Ceci est mon corps,* Neuchâtel/Paris, 1955 (*Cahiers théologiques,* 37). English translation: "This is my Body," in *Essays on the Lord's Supper,* Richmond, 1958, pp. 24 ff. (*Ecumenical Studies in Worship,* n. 1).

2. De Baciocchi, J., S.M., "Le mystère eucharistique dans les perspectives de la bible," in *NRT* 77 (1955), pp. 561–580.

*1956*

3. Vanneste, A., "Bedenkingen bij de scholastieke transsubstantiatieleer," in *Coll BG* 2 (1956) 322–335.

4. Benoit, P., O.P., "The Holy Eucharist," in *Scripture* 8 (1956), pp. 97–108; 9 (1957), pp. 1–14.

*1958*

5. Dupont, J., O.S.B., "Ceci est mon corps, Ceci est mon sang," in *NRT,* 80 (1958), pp. 1025–1041.

6. *Essays on the Lord's Supper* (see n. 1 above). Leenhardt's "This is my Body" preceded by O. Cullmann's essay, "The Meaning of the Eucharist in Primitive Christianity," pp. 5–23.

*1959*

7. De Baciocchi, J., S.M., "Présence eucharistique et transsubstantiation," in *Irenikon* 33 (1959), pp. 139–164.

8. Ghysens, G., O.S.B., "Présence eucharistique et transsubstantiation," in *Irenikon* 33 (1959), pp. 420–435.

9. Schoonenberg, P., S.J., "De tegenwoordigheid van Christus," in *Verbum* 26 (1959), pp. 148–157.

10. ———, "Eucharistie en tegenwoordigheid," in *Heraut van het Heilig Hart,* 89 (1959), pp. 106–111.

11. ———, "Een terugblik—Ruimtelijke, persoonlijke en eucharistische tegenwoordigheid," *Verbum* 26 (1959), pp. 314–327.

12. Strotman, D. T., "L'orthodoxie dans le debat sur la transsubstantiation," in *Irenikon* 33 (1959), pp. 295–308.

13. Thurian, Max, frère de la communauté de Taizé, *L'Eucharistie, Mémorial du Seigneur, Sacrifice d'action de grâce et d'intercession,* Neuchâtel/Paris, 1959. English translation: *The Eucharistic Memorial,* Richmond, 1960, 1961 (*Ecumenical Studies in Worship,* nn. 7, 8).

14. Verbeek, H., S.J., "De sacramentele structuur van de eucharistie," in *Bijdragen* 20 (1959), pp. 345–355.

*1960*

15. Lescrauwaet, J., M.S.C., "Een nieuwe reformatorische studie over de eucharistie als bijdrage tot de christelijke hereniging," in *Jaarboek* (van de Werkgenootschap van katholieke Theologen in Nederland) 1960, pp. 109–124 (exposition and critique of n. 13 above).

16. Schelfhout, O., "Bedenkingen bij een nieuwe transsubstantiatie-leer," in *Coll BG* 6 (1960), pp. 298–320 (critique of n. 3 above).

17. Vanneste, A., "Nog steeds bedenkingen bij de transsubstantieleer," in *Coll BG* 6 (1960) 321–348. (Reply to n. 16 above.)

*1962*

18. Trooster, S., S.J., "De eucharistische werkelijke tegenwoordigheid van Christus in de hedendagse protestants een

katholieke theologie," *Jaarboek* (van de Werkgenootschap van katholieke Theologen in Nederland), 1962, pp. 113–136.

*1963*

19. Galot, J., S.J., "Théologie de la présence eucharistique," in *NRT* 85 (1963), pp. 19–39.

*1964*

20. Fortmann, H., "Ontrust rondon het dogma," *Nederlandse Katholieke Stemmen* 60 (1964), pp. 297–306.

21. De Haes, P., "Praesentia realis," in *Collectanea Mechliniensia* 49 (1964), pp. 133–150.

22. Schoonenberg, P., S.J., "Tegenwoordigheid," in *Verbum* 31 (1964), pp. 395–415.

*1965*

23. Fortmann, H., "Enkele notities bij nieuwe visies op transsubstantiatie en eucharistische presentie," in *Theologie en Zielzorg* (continuation of *Nederlandse Katholieke Stemmen*) 61 (1965), pp. 89–91.

24. Green, H. B., "The Eucharistic Presence: change and/or signification," in *Downside Review* 83 (1965), pp. 32–46. (Appended to this article is a résumé of Charles Davis's "The Theology of Transsubstaniation" from *Sophia* [University of Melbourne], April, 1965.)

25. Mulders, G., S.J., "Eucharistie," in *Verbum* 32 (1965), pp. 122–129.

26. Paul VI, "Mysterium fidei. Litterae encyclicae de doctrina et cultu ss. Eucharistiae," in *AAS* 57 (1965), pp. 753–774.

27. Sonnen, R., S.J., "Transsubstantiatie," in *Verbum* 32 (1965), pp. 223–238.

28. Schillebeeckx, E., O.P., "Christus' tegenwoordigheid in de eucharistie," in *Tijdschrift voor Theologie* 5 (1965), pp. 136–173.

29. Smits, Luchesius, O.F.M. Cap., *Vragen rondom de Eucharistie,* Roermond, 1965.

30. Trooster, S., S.J., "Transsubstantiatie," in *Streven* 18 (1965), pp. 737–744.

*1966*

31. Delmotte, J., "Mysterium Fidei. Recente publicaties over de Eucharistie," in *Coll BG* 12 (1966), pp. 3–25 (critique of nn. 22, 27, 28 and 29 above).

32. Liesting, G., S.S.S., *Het Sacrament der Eucharistie,* Tielt/The Hague, 1966 (*Woord en Beleving,* 23). (Large bibliography.)

33. Schillebeeckx, E., O.P., "Transsubstantiation, Transfinalization, Transfiguration," in *Worship* 40 (1966), pp. 324–338.

34. ———, "De eucharistische wijze van Christus' werkelijke tegenwoordigheid," in *Tijdschrift voor Theologie,* 6 (1966), pp. 359–394.

# CONCLUSION

AT the end of these reflections on the mystery of the Eucharist, we cannot escape the nagging conviction that there are some who will insist that these contemporary writings do not satisfy the mind which seeks to know the "how" of Christ's presence in the Eucharist because of their lack of "objectivity." Some will feel that because these writings reinterpret or even ignore the traditional theological elaboration of the idea of transsubstantiation, they are therefore not suited to the expression of the faith of the Church in Christ's true presence in the Eucharist and the true change which comes about in the consecration. In a sense there is no reply to these objections. The deeper issue in the present confrontation of attitudes is the issue of reality itself; it is the question "What is reality?" And the answer to this question at the present divides thinkers whether they be Catholic or otherwise. One type of mind will seek to find the beginning of an answer in the independent reality of the world as it is experienced, another will begin with the experience itself of the world and analyze reality in terms of the reality of one's experience of the world. The former attitude is characteristic of the more empirical type of thinking which is so characteristic of British and American scholarship. The latter is characteristic of the continental European style of thought, a style influenced by the existentialist movement. Everyone likes to think that he is right and that his point of view is correct and objective. But it does seem that there is a fundamental option operative in the posture which one adopts towards the real, towards the reality of man in the world. The world is real, but man is real, too, as is his experience of a world of persons and things which is essential to his human development. The fact that one chooses to look at the world from the point of view of his own existence in that world is not necessarily a subjectivism. True, the danger of subjectivism is very real, but it is not limited to the existential style of thought. Subjectivism, a self-centered view of the world, is a human temptation rather than a temptation inherent in a given school or style of thought. It is a danger to the thinker whose style is more empirical as well as to the one whose thought is more person-centered. What is important to see is that these different styles of thought have a great deal to say to each other. One stresses the givenness of the world and the controlling reality of that given world. The other stresses the uniqueness of human existence, the fact that a man cannot be treated simply as an object, that a man is, in Marcel's words, "more than his dossier."[1] It stresses the mystery of the human person, the historical character of his existence, his obligation to build his world through his own freedom rather than letting it overwhelm him. One would hope that instead of dividing into hostile camps these two views of the world could engage in a fruitful dialogue for the betterment of the whole human situation.

In the current theological ferment, then, these styles of thought face each other with a tragic hostility. They refer to each other as "irrelevant" or "relativist." It is important to see that both frameworks of thought have an authentic place in the common philosophical and theological endeavor. And the reflection on the mystery of the Eucharist is no exception. When one looks somewhat dispassionately at what the two points of view are saying, one sees that both depart from the same point: the faith of Trent. Both are attempting to develop a theological intelligibility of the mystery of Christ's presence and of the "marvelous and singular conversion" which takes place in the consecration. The language of transsubstantiation states that the substantial reality of bread and wine is changed into the substantial reality of Christ. The language of transsignification states this same fundamental fact, though it sets the faith of Trent into a more specifically sacramental context, into the context of a

1. G. Marcel, *The Mystery of Being.* I: *Reflection and Mystery,* Chicago: 1950, p. 33.

sign-act of Christ. It stresses the fact that the whole of creation is ultimately sacramental, that it has, in God's ordering of creation, a capacity to incarnate the action in which God gives His life to man. The situation of the physical reality of bread and wine in this concrete historical context shows how bread and wine have the symbolic capacity to bear the action of Christ who reveals Himself to the Eucharistic community and to give Himself in the revelation. Transsubstantiation stresses the objectivity of the change of substance. Transsignification stresses the fact that this objective change takes place by the creative word of Christ the sacramental sign-act, an act which is laden with grace meaning because it is Christ's self-revelation and self-giving. Neither the theological elaboration of transsubstantiation nor that of transsignification can pretend to "explain" or "prove" the eucharistic mystery, the "how" of Christ's Eucharistic presence. Only Christ, the gift of the Eucharist, can "explain" or "prove" Himself to man. And that explanation and proof is not a matter of words of human construction. It is only found in the life which Christ shares with His body in this ineffable mystery.

# INDEX

(NUMBERS IN ITALICS REFER TO FOOTNOTES ON THE PAGE INDICATED.)